AF478852

COTTON worldwide

COTTON worldwide

Christina Kleineidam
Hans Peter Jost

Introduction by Pietra Rivoli

Lars Müller Publishers

For Salomé Oriana Miro Noemi

The world's largest cotton producers 2008/2009[*]

[*] Wikipedia; August 2009 (after United States Departement of Agriculture, Foreign Agricultural Service-Production, Supply and Distrubtion Online)
[**] Estimated for 2009/2010 by the International Cotton Advisory Commitee

Introduction

I had been wearing T-shirts, socks, and blue jeans for about forty years before I ever saw a cotton plant. When I first stepped onto a cotton farm near Lubbock, Texas, I was immediately captivated. It was the fall of 2000, and the cotton was open and ready to be stripped. For as far as I could see in any direction, dollops of bright white fluff covered the farmland. It was almost as if tufts of cotton candy had been dropped from the sky. A field of open cotton bolls is a beautiful sight indeed. I bent down to pick a few of these fluffs myself. I put them in my pocket, and took them home to Washington, DC. They sit in my desk drawer today.

That first trip to cotton country did not go exactly as planned. I had timed my visit to coincide with the harvest, and I showed up one morning ready to hop aboard the tractor and see the cotton stripper in action. I was busy, a city girl, and I had taken three days off work to make the trip.

"Well, we won't be stripping cotton today," my host, cotton grower Nelson Reinsch, told me that morning. It had rained a bit the night before, and the cotton was too wet to strip. That night there was another touch of rain, and so the strippers were idle the next day, too. I was not to see the cotton stripping after all, because the cotton needed to dry for a few days before the mechanical stripper could work properly. I went back to Washington empty-handed, so to speak, except for the tufts of cotton in my pocket.

This experience is significant to me even today, because it illustrates the random elements that rule the fortunes of cotton farmers the world over. While white-collar workers might have the luxury of deciding when to schedule meetings or make a phone call, the lives of farmers across the globe are ruled by chance factors that are outside their control. The weather, insects, weeds, or cotton prices: all of these variables take control out of the hands of the cotton farmer and leave his or her fate in the hands of some higher power.

Today, cotton is produced in more than seventy countries in North America, South America, Europe, Asia, and Africa. Remarkably,

cotton is grown in both the richest and poorest countries on earth. A cotton boll from Mali looks much the same as a cotton boll from Texas, but the process by which the cotton is grown differs dramatically. Although cotton farming across the globe shares some basic common aspects, there is also a rank inequality. In the poorest countries, farmers have no protection, nowhere to turn if something goes wrong, while in rich countries a wide variety of supports are in place to help farmers deal with the random elements that can affect their crops. In the USA and the EU, for example, cotton farmers have subsidies to offset unpredictable prices, advanced science to help combat insects, chemicals that can simulate ideal weather conditions, crop insurance to cover losses, and remarkable mechanical technologies to make almost every step in the production process easier. As a result, misfortunes that would be the undoing of cotton farmers in poor countries can be taken in stride by farmers in rich countries. Thanks to science, technology, and government supports, the average American cotton farmer produces more than 400 times as much cotton as his counterpart in West Africa.

This striking imbalance in resources, protection, and hence production is related not only to differences in wealth, but also in political prowess. Farmers in wealthy countries enjoy disproportionate political power, and agricultural interests are often coddled and protected by the more than 99 percent of the population who no longer make their living from the land. In poor countries, however, farmers are normally at the bottom of the chain of political power, and frequently find themselves exploited by the urban elite. Farmers in poor countries also face many challenges that are completely foreign to farmers in rich countries: inadequate transportation, corruption, and illiteracy, to name just a few.

It is difficult to overstate the importance of cotton in world economic history. In the late 1600s, the British—who to this point had been clothed in wool—discovered the wonderfully soft and beautiful cotton fabrics that were produced by hand in India. British consumers could not get enough of these new textiles, which soon threatened the survival of Britain's traditional wool industry. In a fight for survival, the politically powerful wool industry succeeded in banning the import of most cottons from India, forcing Britons back into itchy, expensive clothing.

But once British consumers had tried the inexpensive, soft, and beautiful cotton fabrics, they were no longer content in their woolens. Consumer demand, then as now, was a powerful force that was difficult to tame. Soon after the imports from India were banned, British entrepreneurs developed machines to produce cotton yarn and fabric, and the result was the world's first factories. The mechanical innovations that sparked textile production soon led to all manner of broader industrial development in Britain. Indeed, Joseph Shumpteter wrote that the entire early industrial history of Britain "can be resolved into the history of this single industry." Quite simply, the ignition switch for the Industrial Revolution was the production of cotton textiles.

Thus began the so-called "race to the bottom" that continues today. As the Industrial Revolution led to higher wages in Britain, production shifted to America to take advantage of lower labor costs. The next stop in the race was Japan, followed by Hong Kong, Korea, and Taiwan. Today, China is the world's largest producer of cotton textiles. Throughout its history, this industry has exposed both the promise and the perils of global capitalism.

Perhaps no other industry is so closely associated with the evils of sweatshops. From Charles Dickens' "Satanic mills" to the garment factories of South China today, workers in the textile and apparel trades have long been held up as examples of the exploited, abused, and underpaid. In general, the ideal worker for these industries has been desperate and docile, willing to do mind-numbing work at a backbreaking pace for little pay. Yet for most of economic history the young women who have worked in textile and apparel factories preferred this work to the farm life they left behind, and the factory jobs presented them with a taste of autonomy that had never been possible in a traditional agricultural village. The irony—whether 200 years ago in Britain or in China today—is that exploitation in sweatshops has played a significant role in the liberation of young women. And the cotton textile factories in poor countries today continue to spark broader industrial development.

Cotton farms as well as textile factories have a unique role in labor history. Cotton has traditionally been among the most labor-intensive crops to grow, with large numbers of workers

needed at unpredictable times to plant, weed, and harvest the crop. As the Industrial Revolution took hold in Britain, demand for the fluffy white cotton bolls exploded, and farmers the world over—especially in the USA—expanded their production of cotton. By the mid-ninteenth century, it was the slave plantations in the USA that produced most of the world's cotton. The most horrific chapter of American labor history—as well as the Civil War—can be traced quite directly to the cotton plant.

Today, wealthy countries use barely any labor at all to produce cotton, because virtually every step in the process has been mechanized. In poor countries, however, cotton farming remains powered by human labor. In some countries, this labor operates in a system not too far removed from slavery. In 2008, there were numerous news reports that many schools in Uzbekistan had closed during the cotton harvest, with children being forcibly sent to the fields to handpick cotton.

Perhaps nowhere is the divide between rich and poor cotton farmers more evident than at harvest time. A capable and quick worker can pick about 150 pounds of cotton per day, while the most advanced cotton stripping machine in the USA allows one person to harvest more than 75,000 pounds during the same period. The machine, the John Deere 7760, costs more than half a million dollars, a surreal amount for the typical African cotton farmer, whose income may be less than one dollar per day.

Today, one of the most fascinating and controversial aspects of cotton production relates to environmental sustainability. Cotton farmers have always faced battles with insects, weeds, and weather, but during most of the postwar period, these battles were fought with chemical means, particularly in wealthy countries, but also in poor ones. One chemical herbicide was applied early to keep weeds from sprouting, others were applied later to kill weeds that had already emerged. A variety of pesticides were developed to target cotton's enemy insect, of which there are many. Where cotton is harvested by machine, other chemicals are applied to simulate a freeze, which makes the plant brittle and easier for the machine to strip. Virtually all of these chemicals pose potential threats to water, to people, and to wildlife. And to top it off, cotton is among nature's thirstiest plants,

consuming much of the available freshwater in cotton-growing regions. For obvious reasons, farming practices in the postwar era are typically referred to as "high input" agriculture.

No one would argue that these methods of cotton production are environmentally sustainable. However, there are radically different notions regarding the best way forward. On the one hand, there is the "back to nature" response of those who advocate a return to organic agriculture. There is increasing demand from apparel consumers for organic cotton garments and bedding, and some farmers have responded by returning to natural methods of weed and insect control. Organic cotton farming can now be found throughout the world, from West Texas to West Africa to Turkey.

On the other hand, others argue that saving the planet will require another leap into the future, rather than a step back into the past. During just the past few years, genetic engineering has led to cotton seeds that produce their own natural and benign pesticides, reducing chemical pesticide use in many areas of the USA by more than 80 percent. Similar genetic advances have led to fewer and less harmful herbicide applications. The world's leading agricultural company, Monsanto, has pledged that its scientific advances will double cotton yields by 2030, while reducing energy consumption, land use, and water input by 30 percent.

Whether the protection of our planet is best achieved by accelerating toward the future or by returning to the past, the debate again brings into sharp relief the chasm between rich and poor cotton farmers. In many poor countries, cotton production is de facto organic, because farmers are unable to afford the expensive chemical inputs. In rich countries, however, most farmers look upon science as their salvation, and regard organic farming—with its many unpredictable aspects—as anything but sustainable.

Cotton has many stories to tell: stories about wealth and poverty, about history, science, politics, and the environment. Perhaps most of all, however, cotton tells a story about globalization, since every sock or T-shirt in our wardrobe has its own global history. By the time it reaches the store shelf, a simple T-shirt will typically have traveled to at least three continents. Perhaps it was born on a farm in West Texas, one of the world's most important cotton-growing regions. The cotton then likely traveled to Asia, where the voracious textile industry transformed it into yarn and then fabric and then clothing. Its next journey was probably back to a rich country—perhaps the USA, an EU state, or Japan—where consumer demand for clothing continues to accelerate. Even when it is discarded, the T-shirt's global life story will continue. Clothing tossed away by the rich often emerges in the used-clothing markets of Africa, or sometimes makes its way back to China, where it is shredded and used to create stuffed animals, pillows, or other goods that will once again grace store shelves in the world's rich countries. Cotton is a microcosm of our rapidly globalizing world.

This book both shows and tells cotton's many remarkable stories. Most days, I still look at the cotton bolls that sit in my desk drawer. I love the bright white color, the sweet musty smell, and especially the soft feel of this bit of fluff with its fascinating history.

Pietra Rivoli

Delhi
INDIA
Jaipur
Ahmadabad
Khandwa
Kasrawad
Nagpur
Akola
Mumbai

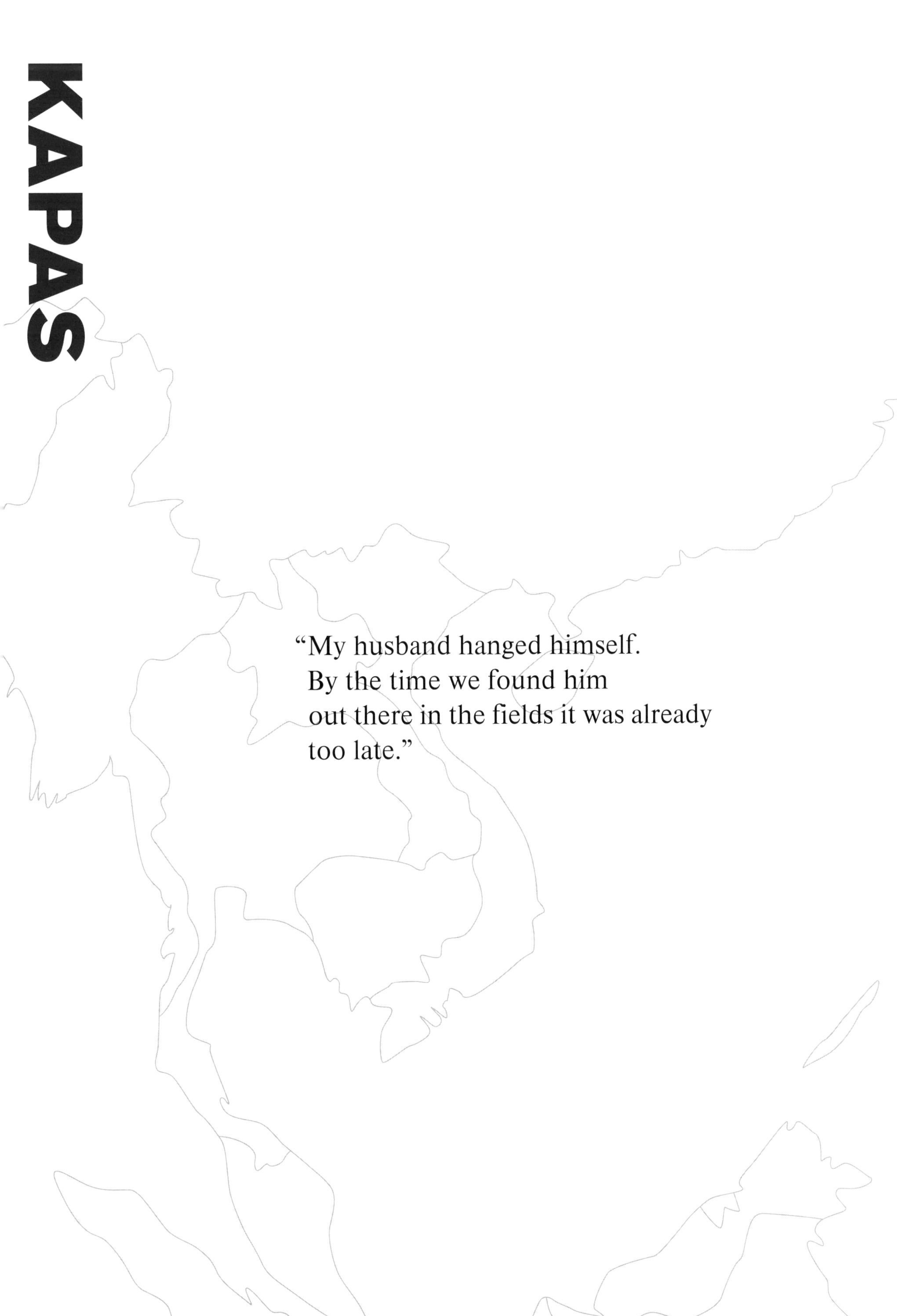

"My husband hanged himself.
By the time we found him
out there in the fields it was already
too late."

"My husband hanged himself. By the time we found him out there in the fields it was already too late." Kusum Jadhao draws one end of her sari over her head in a small gesture made countless times every day. But this time, it is as if she is trying to hide away. She lives with her two sons in Dadham, a small village about 124 miles west of Nagpur, where most of the population are untouchables, at the lower end of the Indian social scale. Although officially abolished, the caste system, which is closely linked with the Hindu faith, still influences life in India today. Kusum's small shack is no different from those of her neighbors: a single, sparsely lit room, with a kitchen in the back. A wooden frame with cotton bands stretched across it serves as a seat. Depending on the time of day, it is also a sofa or bed for those who do not sleep on the ground. The family's few belongings hang on the wall, together with a framed photograph of Sahadio, Kusum's deceased husband. She is forty-three years old; her husband was only a few years older. Her bracelets jangle gently as she takes the photograph down from the wall to show it to us, with an emotionless face that expresses nothing of her tragic fate. "He couldn't go on. There wasn't enough money to pay back the debts to the moneylender. The interest rates increased every year and, when we finally got a loan from the bank, the moneylender no longer wanted the money but the harvest instead. And if that is not enough he'll take our land away from us." The moneylender is as much a part of Indian village life as the water buffalo that stands placidly in the river or puddle. He charges between 50 and 120 percent interest on his loans. The Jadhao family fell into the moneylender's clutches because they faced the kind of problems that are typical among the rural population, problems that only cash can solve quickly.

The most pressing of these is how to make good the loss if a crop fails. A single bad harvest can spell financial ruin: without money there is no seed for the next season, so the farmer is forced to sell the oxen and buffalo he needs to work the fields and which provide milk, dung, and fuel. Dowries pose another financial problem, even though it is officially forbidden to demand one. It is primarily poor and uneducated families who take on this great burden in order to prevent a daughter from remaining unmarried, a state that is seen as dishonorable. Even after the death of her husband, Kusum was unable to free herself of the

Reikha Suradkar, a 30-year-old widow, lives with
her children in Hatola in the Vidarbha region, which
has achieved a tragic notoriety on account of the
large numbers of suicides. Her husband, Hanuman,
killed himself in 2006 by drinking pesticide, as he
was overwhelmed by heavy debts.

usurer. "I didn't even get the 1,500 euros due to me from the state," she says, "as the authorities did not record suicide as the cause of death in the death certificate." Sahadio hanged himself, but the officials in charge of the case chose to ask the money-lender of all people what the certified cause of death should be. Kusum is suing him but is unwilling to give us his name.

Dadham is in the Vidarbha region of the state of Maharashtra, part of India's cotton belt, which the press polemically refer to as the "Suicide Belt." Over the past ten years there have been ten thousand such suicides throughout India, a thousand of them in Maharashtra alone. There is nothing to indicate that these acts of desperation are abating, and the problem is so serious that the government saw itself forced to take action and decided to make a one-time payment of 1,500 euros to the dependents of the deceased. The grotesque consequence of this has been that despairing farmers often see suicide as a last chance to help their families get even a small amount of money. The belief in rebirth certainly plays a role here, although in the Hindu faith suicide leads to bad karma in the next life.

For Kusum and her children little has changed. She still plants cotton, soybeans, and corn in her field, which is only about two acres in size. The success of her crops depends on the monsoon rains, because she cannot afford the pumps and pipes that would give her access to artificial irrigation. One person who can afford them is a big local farmer for whom Gangaran, the younger of her two sons, works for seventy cents a day, for up to five months of the year if he is lucky. "My son left school because he felt guilty about not being able to contribute to the upkeep of the family," his mother explains with a tired smile, but visibly proud of her son. Before we bid her farewell we ask what she wishes for the future. "Justice! And work for my sons."

The aid organization YUVA (Youth for Unity and Voluntary Action) is trying to combat suicides among the cotton farmers. With the backing of Swissaid and a lot of voluntary helpers, YUVA carries out educational work and offers advice on the purchase of seed and the cultivation of fields. "Most of these people are illiterate," explains Suresh Lule, one of the workers. "Try explaining to them what genetically manipulated seed is.

What counts here is what the men discuss among themselves in the tearoom. They all exaggerate their successes a little, and there is no objectivity—that's men for you!" He is referring to the problem with BT-1, a genetically manipulated variety of cotton that farmers in India have been permitted to sow since 2002. Nana Patekar, a highly acclaimed Indian movie star, made TV commercials for this product, which is marketed by the American chemical concern Monsanto, together with the Indian company Mahyco. "He promised rich harvests for happy families who would live in beautiful houses," a message that traveled from the glittering world of the Indian film industry to the few television sets in Central India and which definitely had an impact: the farmers bought the expensive tins of seed and dreamed of a better future.

The companies built certain genes from *Bacillus thuringiensis,* a soil bacterium, into the genetic makeup of BT-1 to produce BT toxin, which is deadly to bollworms, a dreaded cotton pest. Monsanto succeeded in identifying the gene that is responsible for this poison in the genetic material of the bacterium and was able to transfer it to the cotton gene. This resulted in the first genetically manipulated variety of cotton that is able to produce the toxin on its own and thus reduce the use of expensive pesticides. This is the theory, but in practice it has only been partially borne out. The range of disadvantages that YUVA noted in field studies conducted in the Vidarbha region is seemingly endless: the high-tech seed is expensive and, as it is a hybrid, has to be bought new every year. "Many farmers didn't know this and they simply sowed the sterile seed the following season." Apparently, the star of the TV commercials forgot to mention this detail. The bollworm has indeed vanished for the most part, but other pests, the bollworm's natural enemies, are multiplying rapidly in its absence. The result is that pesticides are still necessary despite everything, and instead of saving money, the farmers are faced with additional costs. There is also an increased need for water, an important detail the tins do mention, but then which of the farmers, if any, can read this information?

Taraboi Dungeree, who is forty, no longer knows what kind of cotton her husband sowed. In 2004, at the age of forty-five, he hanged himself, as he, too, had debts with a moneylender. Now his widow has to raise five chldren alone. Fortunately, she has just one daughter, whose dowry will not be due for a few years yet. By the time Taraboi and her sons have returned from the fields, half of the inhabitants of the village of Mahagao are already gathered around her hut, which is set in a carefully swept courtyard with a tamped earth floor. The village teacher has also hurried over to speak on behalf of this reserved woman who silently welcomes us into her home. "Taraboi and another widow went to Delhi for an audience with Dr. Abdul Kalam, the Indian president at the time," he tells us proudly. With the help of YUVA the two women, who had never left the village before in their lives, summoned up enough courage to draw attention to themselves and to the fate of other widows. Taraboi received the one-time payment from the state. Her husband left behind two oxen and a scant two acres of land, on which conventional cotton is now in full blossom. If everything goes according to plan she will get between 500 and 600 euros for it, the only cash that the family of six will have until the next harvest.

After our visit with Taraboi, the teacher insists that we visit his school. The loud cheers of the children accompany us along the dusty path there, past small shacks with fenced enclosures for oxen, goats, and chickens. The village is poor, with neither shops nor a tearoom, and only a few trees to offer shade. In the classroom the children rapidly form a group, each of them gazing at us expectantly. The statue of a Hindu god on a small altar has been freshly painted with yellow and red pigment and is surrounded by flowers, and above the blackboard hangs a picture of Mahatma Gandhi, seated with his legs crossed and spinning on his *charkha*, a traditional hand-operated spinning wheel. Cotton played an important role in the philosophy of this "great soul," as he is respectfully called, for *khadi*, the handspun and handwoven cotton fabric, was to be self-produced and worn by every Indian, a utopian ideal that sought to establish material and intellectual independence. Independence from the British colonial rulers, from the state in general, and from the influence of other cultures. As India's villages—home to 80 percent of the population of the subcontinent—were least exposed to such influences, it was here that Gandhi saw the opportunity for the nation's future.

Sixty years after Gandhi's death, what is the message to the children in these villages, children whose fathers are committing suicide for lack of an infrastructure, because of inadequate education or the fact that they belong to a low caste, in the face of profit-greedy national and international corporations and the subvention policies of Europe and America? The USA distributes between three and four billion dollars annually among the highly industrialized cotton farmers of America, which results in falling prices worldwide. As farmers in the developing and emerging nations have to make do without any form of subsidy, let alone a state-guaranteed minimum price, planting cotton is becoming less and less profitable for them, and many have to change over to other agricultural products. European and American subventions for agricultural products are to be abolished in 2013, following protests from Brazil, Mali, and three other West African producers, who formed an alliance to take the matter to the arbitration court of the World Trade Organization (WTO).

The children in the classroom of Mahagao know nothing about all this. We draw Switzerland's mountains on the blackboard as we tell them about the Indian cotton that is spun in Switzerland and the Swiss machines that are used in India. And about Heidi—which turns out to be the most popular topic of all.

Mahatma Gandhi, wrapped in *khadi* and leaning on his walking stick, can be found on many public squares in India. The statues of the little man seem to trace his protest marches through the country, as well as his nonviolent resistance to the British colonial rulers, which ultimately led to independence in 1947. In Khandwa, a cotton center south of the industrial city of Indore, Gandhi smiles as he gazes at the oxcarts on their way to the cotton market and at the trucks, fully loaded with bales of pressed cotton fibers, leaving for the cotton gins which will separate the fiber and seed. Most of them are heading in the direction of Tamil Nadu, the new "Indian Manchester," or will be shipped to the textile centers of Asia. The marketplace is a large walled square. The carts stand in rows along raised platforms, and the oxen rest beside them, contentedly chewing their cud. Hoof trimmers wait for customers and dusty farmers wash themselves and their laundry in the animals' drinking troughs. Jitendra Arone is one such farmer. "Our farm is six miles from here," he tells us over a cup of tea. He is exhausted from the first stage of his journey, but also excited and eager for the money that he will soon have in his hands. Although he had to set off from home in the middle of the night, he enjoys the journey to the city. "This year we harvested 17,600 pounds of cotton, on seven and a half acres of land," he informs us. Suddenly, the crowd starts to move, as the buyers from the gins have arrived. Like the others, Jitendra quickly opens up his load and pulls it apart, down to the lowest layers, so that samples can be taken from all the layers: fiber length 28 millimeters, high tensile strength. After a brief period of bargaining, both sides agree on a price: 33.90 euros per quintal (220 pounds). An official from the Indian Cotton Corporation checks that the minimum price is not undercut. At the end of 2006, this stood at 33.70 euros per quintal. After deducting the costs of seed, fertilizer, and pesticides this means a profit of about 28 euros for Jitendra and his family.

Other farmers, about 4,900 of them at the moment, do not have to make their way to the market as their harvest is collected in the village and transported directly to the gin. They work together with bioRe, a Swiss business that has been marketing organic cotton from India since 1991 and from Tanzania since 1994. bioRe is a pioneer in this area and, over the last sixteen years, has developed an efficient system of collaboration in the Nimar region near Kasrawad. "Once a month our staff visit the farmers to discuss everything that is to be done; from sowing to fertilizing to natural pest control, if necessary," explains Rajeev Baruah, the head of the training center. The farmers are also provided with seed. "Certified organic seed doesn't exist yet. All we can do is check that it has not been chemically treated. If Europe ever introduces stricter certification standards, something will have to be done here." The buyers pay a surcharge of 10 to 15 percent on the current daily price. This is possible because the people who buy organic cotton are willing to pay a high price and demand is increasing. Environmental organizations point with increasing urgency to the water problem and the contamination caused by pesticides in the worldwide production of cotton. Health risks for producers are increasing and consumers are also coming into contact with pesticides in the finished product. Trendsetters such as Nike and Adidas are now taking this into account, having also noted that organic cotton is good for their image.

Planting organic cotton is in harmony with the traditions of Indian agriculture: farmers sow local cotton varieties, which have adapted to the climate and soil conditions, and their animals provide the necessary fertilizer. At bioRe's neat and tidy training center, the staff are even taking a first step in the direction of biodynamics, which is compatible with the ayurvedic way of thinking. "As money does not have to borrowed to buy expensive BT seed and the requisite chemicals, the financial vulnerability of the families is reduced," says Mr. Baruah, addressing the problem of debt, which also affects farmers in this part of the cotton belt. But it is not just a question of reducing debt. The foundation that set up bioRe also promotes development in the local community of farmers and gives loans to help build up the infrastructure—for biogas plants or water storage systems, for example.

Studies such as those conducted by YUVA have demonstrated that the use of BT cotton is not a viable long-term alternative for the small farmer. The high production costs drive many of them into the clutches of moneylenders. The organic cultivation of local cotton varieties is a slower, yet ecologically and economically more sustainable, method for a better future.

For Reikha Suradkar, an attractive thirty-year-old from Hatola, this future is not yet within view. Her husband, Hanuman, died in October 2006 at the age of only thirty-five. Their children, two of them girls, are still small. "He drank pesticide while he was out in our field. After we found him he managed to stay alive for a few days, but he never recovered." The recorded cause of death was mental illness. The tragedy of this young family began ten years before his suicide. At that time they had to take out a loan of 500 euros. The interest rate was 50 percent, money that was never available. "The moneylender visited us regularly," Reikha recalls. "This pressure provoked bouts of depression and panic attacks in my husband." A second loan, this time from a bank and with only 10 percent interest, came too late to help. Only since 2007 has it been possible for farmers to get bank loans on simplified terms. Large advertising posters in the cities inform those who can read about these loans. The young widow has to work her land alone, without help and without state subsidies. She has only one hope: a lawyer is trying to prove that

Hanuman Namdu's death was suicide. As a result, she would at least receive the 1,500 euros the government has pledged to pay the dependents of suicide victims. When? "Perhaps in ten years' time," the lawyer says. "The courts in India are slow, and time is elastic." And the moneylender's name? Silence.

Kusum Jadhao's 43-year-old husband took his life in 2004, as the harvest was never enough to pay back the debts to the moneylender. Dadham, Vidarbha region

"Most of these people are illiterate.
Try explaining to them what genetically
manipulated seed is!"

In an audience with President Dr. Abdul Kalam, Taraboi
Dungeree, 40, drew attention to the widows of farmers who
had committed suicide. The NGO YUVA supported this
woman, who left her village for the first time to meet with
the president. Mahagao, Vidarbha region

The large numbers of suicides in the state of Maharastra led to the decision to make a one-time payment to the bereaved. The 1,500 euros were paid in 2005 to Bhikaji Nagoji, 48, mother of three adult sons. Choripagar, Vidarbha region

In November 2006, workers demonstrated against the
closing of the Century Textile Industry, one of the
last textile factories in central Mumbai, which was slated
to be shut down at the end of the year. High property
prices in the city center drive the factories out to cheaper
areas, often in the states of Gujarat and Tamil Nadu.

Many families who have lost their land through debts
go to find work in the cities. Huts such as these in
a Mumbai slum—very close to the city's Bollywood film
industry—are often all they can afford.

The Madukar brothers own the largest farm in Kanchanpur.
One member of this prosperous family is the mayor of
the village, and another runs the private school, which the
family set up. Vidarbha region

There have been 1,000 suicides in the Vidarbha region
alone and 100,000 in India as a whole over the last
ten years. An improvement of conditions is not in sight.

Khandwa lies in the fruitful Narmada Valley,
south of Indore. The city is an important trading
center for cotton.

The farmers with their oxen and carts travel
up to nine miles to the big cotton market
in Khandwa and then, like this couple, wait for
hours for the buyers to arrive.

Staff members of the Swiss firm bioRe collect the harvest
from farms more than nine miles away from the gin
in Kasrawad. This is just one of the advantages that the
farmers have from collaborating with the Swiss.

Offerings to the gods ensure successful business deals.
Khandwa

Samples to determine quality and price are taken from
the load. An official of the Indian Cotton Corporation
makes sure that the minimum price, which in December
2006 was four euros per 220 pounds, is adhered to.
Khandwa

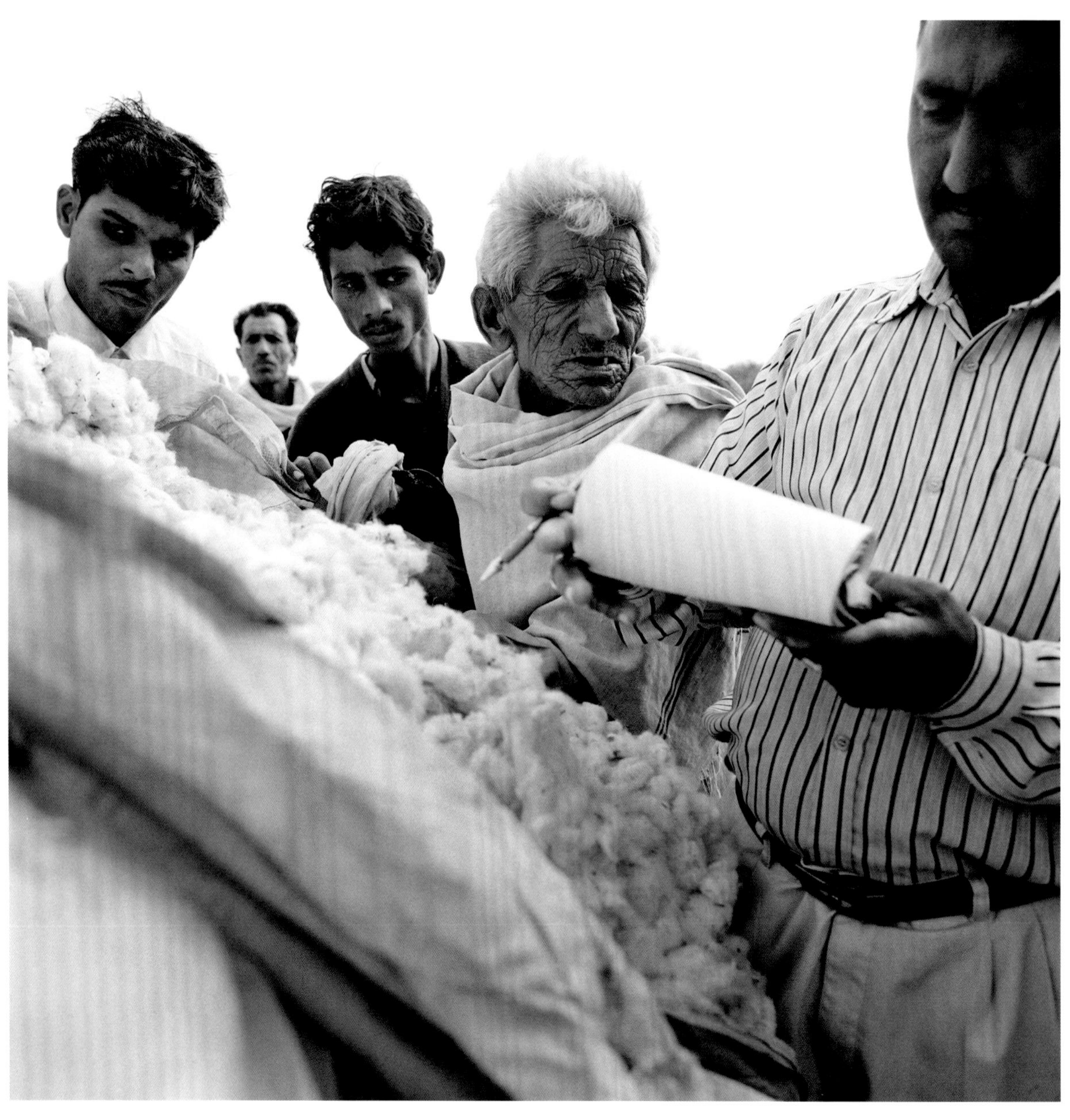

The farmers wait tensely in the bioRe gin for
the purchase manager, Vasudeo Bajad, to announce
the price for their raw cotton. Kasrawad

In this gin a great deal of work in separating the seeds from the cotton fibers must still be done by hand, which is no longer necessary in modern facilities. In India the seeds are generally used to produce animal feed. Khandwa

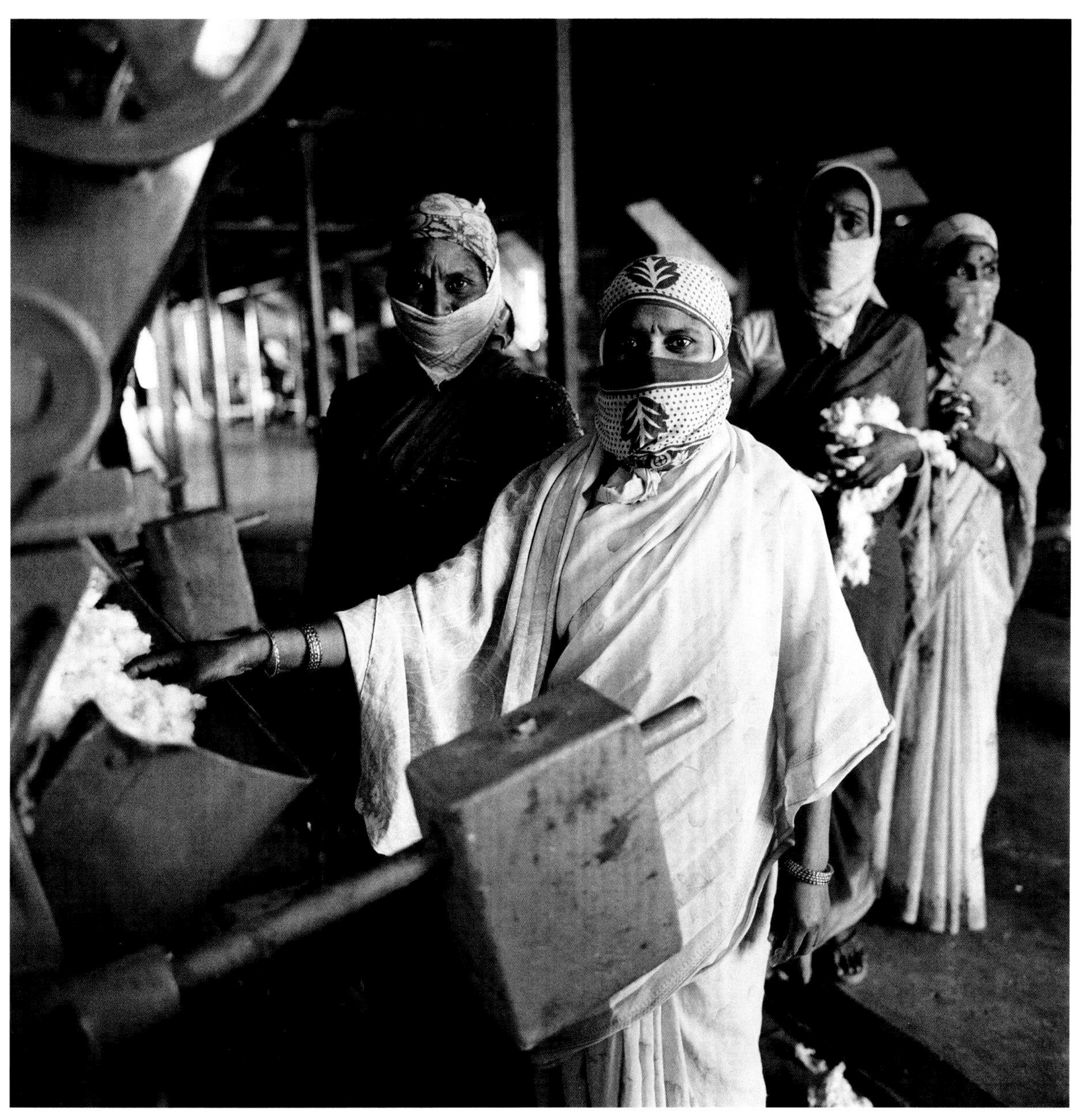

Workers protect their lungs from dust and fiber particles.
Deoli, Wardha district

After ginning, the bales, each around 407 pounds, are weighed
and loaded by hand to be transported to Madras. A buyer notes
down the number and weight of the bales. Khandwa

Ahmadabad, in the state of Gujarat, was once the
"Manchester of India." Today many textile factories have
failed to adapt to the development of technology.

Each region of India has its own textile history. Bagru is
known for cotton saris, whose traditional pattern is made by
block printing: colors are printed over each other using
wooden blocks in a series of stages. Near Jaipur, Rajastan

Aralsee
Mujnak
UZBEKISTAN
Nukus
Chiwa
Aydarkul-
See
Taschkent
Namangan
Andijan
Buchara
Pakhtakor
Zizzach
Fergana
Samarkand

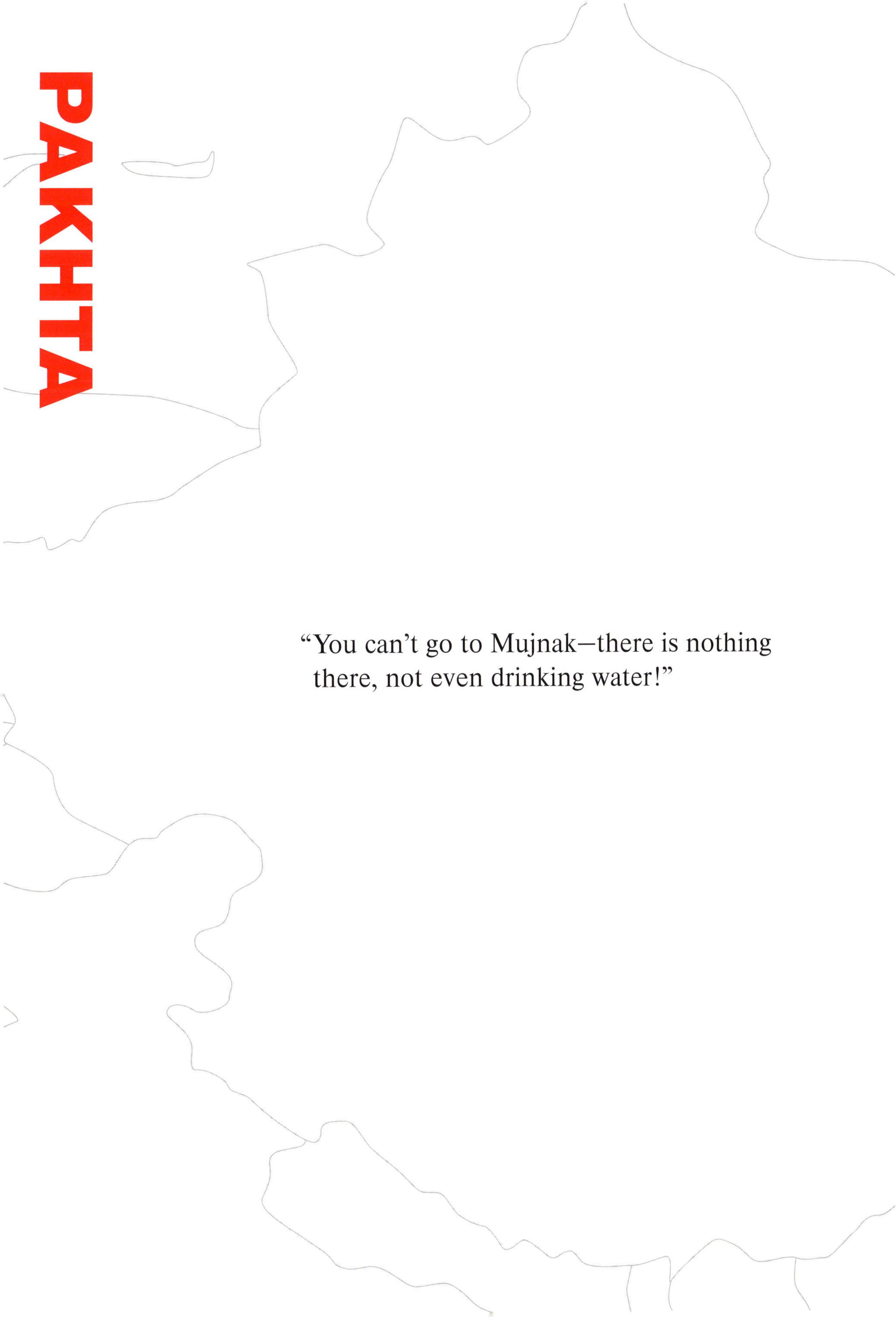

PAKHTA

"You can't go to Mujnak—there is nothing
there, not even drinking water!"

In 1968, twenty-year-old Juraiev Khoshimovich received an enticing offer: in the Sardar Steppe, about 93 miles southwest of Tashkent, land was to be made arable for cotton plantations. The monthly wage of 270 rubles was "an enormous sum of money," he recalls, "and so I didn't spend much time debating and signed on for ten years." The young Uighur left his home in the Fergana Valley, one of Uzbekistan's most fruitful regions, and went to the Hunger Steppe. There was nothing there, just pioneers like him, who lived in yurts and tackled the enormous task of digging a canal to direct the waters of the Syr Darya. Forty years later, a dead-straight road extends through seemingly endless cotton fields. It leads past cotton-stripping works and places such as Pakhtakor or Gagarin, small settlements of precast panel buildings that are no different than other places in the former Soviet Union. *Pakhta* means cotton, *pakhtakor* cotton picker, and this summer, once more, the pickers wait for buses and trucks to take them to the cotton plantations. Their faces wrapped up against the cold of the early morning, they sit at the local bus station under a large mosaic, whose Socialist Realist style glorifies cotton, the white gold of Uzbekistan, and the pickers who work in the fields for the common good—or rather, for the good of those who represent the common people, for in this respect nothing has changed in Uzbekistan, which became an independent republic in 1991.

Juraiev Khoshimovich remained in the Hunger Steppe, like many of his colleagues at the time. He married a woman from the region, had seven children with her, and rose to become the director of a collective farm. "From 1991 onwards I was the elected representative of the private growers of our *shirkat,*" he says, explaining the first reform moves that were introduced after the end of Soviet rule. Now he is retired and pursues a number of private business interests. Juraiev is regarded as someone who knows the desert well, and he is more than willing to accompany us to Aydarkul, the largest of the newly created salt lakes of Uzbekistan, very close to Pakhtakor. He travels over the sand dunes with practiced skill, adroitly avoiding the low saxaul trees that more or less constitute all the flora here. "I am going to lease 25,000 acres of land here and herd sheep and cattle on a commission basis: 37 cents per animal!" He points to the monotonous landscape that surrounds us: sand and saxaul as far

Intensive irrigation leads to an increase in the salt
content of the soil, which then becomes barren. Cotton
field near Mujnak, Karakalpakstan

as the horizon. "Or I will build a harbor! The water will come automatically," he adds, amused at our amazement.

Cotton was already being planted in Central Asia when Russia was still ruled by the czars, but in 1924 Stalin decided to make what is today Uzbekistan into the cotton supplier of the Soviet Union, a decision that was to completely unbalance the hydrological system of the nearby Amu Darya river to the south and the Syr Darya to the north. Thousands of miles of canals have been built since then to exploit the water of Central Asia's two main rivers for huge monocultures. In desert areas with arid and semi-arid climates, artificial irrigation has a tradition dating back to antiquity. In the tenth century BC, water from the oasis city Samarkand was brought in open, lead-lined channels to the fields, where fruit trees, grapes, vegetables, and melons flourished—plants that can easily deal with the natural salt content of arid soils. Problems did not begin until it was decided to use the desert itself for purposes of cultivation, in particular for cotton, one of the most demanding and thirstiest of cultivated plants. Intensive irrigation leads to an increase in the salt content of the soil; the water table level rises, and mineral salts dissolved in water are brought to the upper layers of the soil through the capillary effect, reaching a concentration level that plants cannot tolerate. To wash out the salts the land is regularly flooded, once again with precious freshwater that later, enriched with salt, fertilizer, and pesticides, is led off into the hollows of the desert. Here, new salt lakes form, much like the Aydarkul, although its origins and size are the result of yet another main emphasis of Soviet water management. In 1969, the Chardarya dam that controlled the water level of the reservoir of the same name could no longer contain the floods of the Syr Darya. Valuable masses of freshwater poured through the opened floodgates into the salt hollow of Arnasoy and formed the lake, which since then has been fed by the surplus water from the reservoir. Juraiev has known it since the first puddle formed in the desert sand. "Soon another part of the lake will develop here," he murmurs as he drives carefully through a large wet area. And a little later it emerges, the largest salt lake in Uzbekistan, with an area of 1,160 square miles, lying like a shining mirror in front of us, in the midst of the desert of Kyzylkum. The water that collects here actually belongs in the Aral Sea, and the beauty of the landscape seems like a macabre offer of compensation for this ecological catastrophe. Nearby, a large wall dams freshwater from the Syr Darya, which comes in a canal from Kazakhstan: "To mix fresh and salt water," Juraiev knows, "down to a salinity level that the cotton can tolerate. Then it can be planted here, too."He strokes his pointed white beard reflectively and adjusts his square cap so that it sits properly on his head. It is embroidered with magical lucky charms for him, his family, and their future. And he is convinced—for how could it be otherwise, given all these economic opportunities?—that the future will be a good one.

At dusk, the fishermen living on the banks of the lake draw their nets ashore. The catch is a good one, pike perch, carp, catfish, and other varieties that are sent to all parts of Uzbekistan, to Turkey, and even to Iran. This project is also part of Juraiev's business plan: "Soon we'll build a fish-canning factory here," he says. The fishermen work for him, as he holds the concession for this district. They live in portable buildings erected on the shore. Not far away is a hut, in which mutton for *polov*, a fatty stew with vegetables and rice, is simmering in a large iron pan. One by one, the men finish their work and warm themselves with green tea and coffee. Behind the portable buildings a few of them are saying their evening prayers. Then the vodka bottle is passed around and Juraiev has to join in. Later, on the way back through the nighttime desert, he promptly loses his way and gets stuck several times in sand dunes. "It is a tradition to take a different route on the return journey," he says in an attempt to distract us. But he knows the desert and manages to bring us home, along with the fish that completely fill the trunk of the car. They are fried in the middle of the night. They taste wonderful—despite everything!

Unlike Juraiev, the members of the Holdorov family have never left the Fergana Valley. "Our district won first place again this year: best quality, largest quantity!" The eldest son, Abdugaffor, proudly summarizes the quotas of the state cotton harvest that are published daily. Uzbekistan is the fifth-largest cotton producer worldwide and the second-largest exporter of cotton. Satisfied, he takes his cell phone out of the pocket of his brand-new suit. "Yes, I'll pick it up this afternoon," he says to the car dealer

at the other end. He is about to fulfill the dream of all Uzbeks:
an Uzbek Daewoo Matiz costs around 6,000 euros, a fortune in
a country where many families must manage on about 25 euros
a month. "That's last year's profit," he says, beaming. "Honestly,
we've been much better off ever since we gained independence."

Opinions are divided on this matter in the sixteen-year-old republic. Karimov, the first and so far only president, rules with an
iron fist, but this is accepted by many of his countrymen, for
"that was the way with Genghis Khan and Tamerlane." The he-
raldic animal on Uzbekistan's national emblem is the mythical
Semurg bird, ringed with cotton bolls and wheat ears. According
to legend, "He whose head it settles on will become king." In
December 2007, it landed on the head of the president once
again, for the third time, despite the constitution's two-term
limit. Nevertheless, Uzbeks do not like to link Karimov personally with the corruption that has increased in the country since
the end of Soviet rule. On the contrary, he is celebrated as a
reformer. His critics, on the other hand, see the backward steps
that the country is taking: no milk for the childen, inadequate
medical services, and poor schooling. "During the Soviet era
every gifted pupil was assisted," says a diplomatic representative in Tashkent. "Today, we have difficulty in finding suitable
candidates for the existing scholarships. Those who have no
money learn less, diplomas are bought, and whoever can afford
it studies abroad."

Abdugaffor did not have to study abroad, for his father, Akmal,
worked in the Namangan district *hokymiat*, in the department
responsible for agriculture, both before and after independence.
The *hokym* is at the pinnacle of the administrative hierarchy; he
can be the mayor or the local district head. Each *hokym* is named
by his direct superior; at the highest level this means by the
president personally. Akmal Holdorov must have been on good
terms with his *hokym,* as he was among the first in the region to
be allowed to lease land: 250 acres for a period of fifty years.
"That was ten years ago," his son recalls. "We had to have a tractor, that was the condition." This detail in the land reform of 1993
excluded the great majority of the farmers from the very start,
for who in those days had his own tractor? The Holdorovs now
own three and have their land cultivated by the members of the

twenty families who lived on Xoldorbek, the name of the collective farm, during the Soviet era. "Two families each share a two and a half acres of land on which they can cultivate whatever they want, either to meet their own needs or to sell at the market," says Abdugaffor, explaining the land reform system. The only other way for these farmers to earn cash is during the cotton harvest: a grown man can manage between 176 and 220 pounds a day, the picking wage being about two cents per kilo of raw cotton. It is the same rate for everyone, including the fifty day workers, the pupils, and the students who strengthen the team of the Holdorovs during the harvest period.

Abdugaffor studied agriculture, and yet the *hokymiat* still tells him how to run his business. He must plant eighty-five acres of cotton using the newly developed cotton variety Buchara 103, which needs less water, and he must sell the entire harvest to the state at a fixed price. If he does not meet the prescribed target, his family will have to hand back the land, a risk that the Holdorovs (and not only they) try to avoid by using large doses of fertilizer and pesticides. The production and marketing of these has been privatized and lies in the hands of the elite close to the government who are not interested in reducing this input of chemicals. "If I had the choice, I wouldn't plant cotton, but rice or wheat instead," a wish that other farmers share. Even after the designated quota has been sold to the state, there is enough rice or wheat left for sale at private markets, where prices can be up to 250 percent higher than those paid by the state.

On the way from Namangan to Tashkent, we are able to convince ourselves of the legendary fertility of the Fergana Valley. Wherever we go, we come across fields of cotton ready to be picked, impressive in their white richness. Many of these fields are lined by poplars, a traditional method of lowering the water table level that we will later encounter in China's Xinjiang Province. Poplars are thirsty. The water absorbed by their roots evaporates through the leaves, which ensures a high level of air humidity and, in turn, counteracts the drying out of the ground. Mulberry trees also fulfill this function. Raising silkworms and producing Atlas silk is one of the handicraft traditions of Uzbekistan that is slowly beginning to flourish once more.

In Mingbulak, a small roadside town, it is the weekly market day. There is a traffic jam, not because of the market itself but because, by order of the authorities, it is not taking place. Angry visitors are talking to the policemen who have to implement this order. In the shadow of the bus station sit officials who recruit cotton pickers and send them as soon as possible in military convoys to those fields in which the harvesting is the most urgent.

60 percent of Uzbeks live in the countryside. Of these, 70 percent are among the nation's poorest people. There is no freedom of choice regarding place of residence; families must live where they have been registered. Unemployment has been high since the end of Soviet rule, as many state business were closed down. In spite of all this, working with cotton is not popular: it is hard work and poorly paid. Every year, it is hard for cotton farmers to find enough pickers at the right time. The *hokym*, where applications for workers must be made, recruits students and schoolchildren, who are compelled to work in the fields from the age of fourteen. As was customary in the Soviet era, universities and schools outside the capital remain closed during the harvest. "At the beginning it's relatively easy to pick 30 pounds, but towards the end of the harvest period it gets increasingly hard," says our driver, Firdauz, recalling his student years. He always bought cotton from the farmers in order to meet the planned target and to avoid the risk of public humiliation.

"But you could also get to know girls more easily during harvest time," he says, weighing up the hard life with a certain sentimentality in his voice. He comes from a Muslim family, and has been going to the mosque on Fridays and fasting during the month of Ramadan since he turned eighteen.

"I'm allowed take part for the first time," fourteen-year-old Ilaja tells us proudly in English. She is hardly taller than the plants that she picks cotton from. Like many children away from their family for the first time, she sees the work in the fields and the accommodation in gym halls or schools as a kind of holiday camp, and is pleased at the chance to earn some money. Ilaja waits for her lunch in the shade of the mulberry trees at the edge of the fields, while other children sit under the canopies they have stretched between the cotton plants. The teachers, who also work in the fields during harvest, warm up *lagman*, the typical Uzbek noodle soup, and distribute *nan*, the round bread. One of the older students comes over to us, curious. He is the champion of his group, easily picking 220 pounds a day, "but I don't always get the money for my work," he says in a low voice while glancing in the direction of his teacher. The latter is nervous because the director is coming, and we have to leave. "No photographs allowed," we are suddenly told. In the car we learn why. "The director and the teachers keep part of the money for themselves. It was the same in my day," Firdauz tells us, lowering his voice even though we are traveling alone with him.

With a certain resignation he pays bribes at arbitrary police checks along the way so as not to lose his driver's license. He tries to lighten this depressing reality with a pinch of humor: "Why are there so many policemen on public squares in Uzbekistan? Because there aren't enough public squares!" All officials need to earn extra money: policemen earn one hundred euros a month, teachers earn sixty. Firdauz is twenty-eight years old and more than willing to take advantage of the opportunities that the growth in tourism offers him. His capital is his carefully cultivated English and a car that is even better looked after. He has been a father for two weeks. His son's name is Ahmed, "without the Uzbek 'r' that no Chinese can pronounce," he says, already thinking of his son's professional future! But he sees him only rarely, as he is constantly traveling back and forth across the country with different customers. He is content with his life: "I want to buy another apartment in Tashkent"—he already has two— "it's a safe investment, as all Uzbeks want to live in the capital." Paying a bribe of 2,000 dollars to the officials at the local registration authority will make this possible, despite all legal restrictions on changing one's place of residence and the lack of a work contract.

Mrs. Izrailbekova in Tashkent is most upset: "You cannot spend the night in Mujnak," she tells us during one of her many phone calls. "There is nothing there! No hotels, not even drinking water!" Even though she has never been there, she knows what she is talking about. She also knows what is good for foreigners: the oasis towns along the legendary Silk Road, with mosques and madrassas, restored and rebuilt for a growing number of tourists and as a means for the independent Republic of Uzbekistan to find its identity. Tamerlane (Timur the Lame), or Emir Timur as people here prefer to call him, for a lame national hero does not seem right, has replaced the monuments of Stalin and Karl Marx. Although he was a Mongol, not an Uzbek, Tamerlane serves as an identification figure from a glorious past. His vast empire extended from Mongolia across India all the way to the shores of the Mediterranean. During the Soviet era, the very mention of his name was forbidden. Stalin wanted to eradicate all memories of the old times and arbitrarily redrew the borders of Russian Turkistan to create the five Central Asian republics of Uzbekistan, Kazakhstan, Kyrgyzstan, Tajikistan, and Turkmenistan, which later became independent within these borders. Railway lines are now interrupted by national borders, where officials demand entry visas; power stations on the upper reaches of the Syr Darya compete for the precious water with cotton plantations on the lower stretches; foodstuffs and natural resources are used to bring in currency instead of to meet the needs of the population.

With the recommendations of the tourist expert and despite her less than encouraging information about the former Aral Sea port, we travel westward along the old Silk Road, an asphalt track with potholes that confidently calls itself a highway. As in the days of Marco Polo, it leads through the deserts that make up sixty percent of the country: the red Kyzylkum in the north, the black Kara-Kum in the south, and finally the new, highly contaminated Aralkum, which has developed where the Aral Sea once was. It is in Karakalpakstan, one of the poorest regions of the country and that most severely affected by the ecological catastrophe: of every thousand children here, ninety die as a result of pulmonary illnesses and poor nutrition. During the journey through the bare landscape, the sudden transition from unirrigated to irrigated land repeatedly attracts our attention. The yellow-red of the deserts and semi-deserts yields to the luxuriant green of the cotton plants, as if borders had been drawn with a ruler. A main canal, through which the water of the Amu Darya is pumped into the desert, is always within sight. Leading off from the main canal is an ever-present network of open concrete channels, often defective and with leaks from which water gushes uselessly into the landscape. The museum in the town of Nukus attempts to convey an impression of how the Amu Darya delta once looked: a large area of water dotted with many islands, with jungle-like flora and fauna. It was replaced by large irrigation areas for the cotton and rice that flank the last 155 miles of our journey to Mujnak. The deterioration in the quality of the soil visibly increases towards the north, with fewer and fewer plants holding out against the high salt content of the earth. Finally, shortly before our goal, nothing more grows and the salt crust that spreads along the furrows breaks like ice beneath one's feet.

Mujnak does not seem like a city that once had a population of 30,000, where fishing and the fish-processing industry brought prosperity, where spa guests lived in sanatoriums, and where one could go bathing even in November. The airport, from which flights once left for the entire Soviet Union, has long since sanded up, and the only signs of life are around the bus station. Housed in containers, a pharmacy, two small shops, and a bar offer their goods. The few tourists Firdauz brings here generally just make a brief visit to photograph the famous boats that lie in the sand, slowly rusting away. This makes us all the more astonished to discover that there are, in fact, two local hotels, but all the rooms are taken by a couple of hundred Chinese looking for oil and gas deposits. The word quickly gets around that we are looking for somewhere to stay. Women discuss who could put us up, and one of them finally squeezes into the car. Her teeth are covered with gold—"good for the stomach," she later explains. She directs Firdauz to the apartment building in which she lives and which looks as if it has been discarded somewhere outside of this town that has nothing urban about it. Small houses of various styles line the sandy, unpaved roads, revealing something about the people from Russia, Poland, and Ukraine who were banished here in pre-Soviet times. Fences made of woven reeds protect the properties against the wind, which has grown increasingly strong since the Aral Sea disappeared.

Orasgul is the name of our host. She is forty-three and has six children. "My husband is dead, but two of my sons live in Kazakhstan and send me money," she tells us while she serves green tea. Many Uzbeks look for work on plantations in Kazakhstan or on Russian building sites, although they generally work there illegally. Of the other children, only five-year-old Umida and eleven-year-old Dinara are at home, listening to the latest music hits on the new stereo system—cranked up to full volume, like everywhere else in Uzbekistan. Inquisitive, they sit with us on the floor where we will later eat and sleep. Even though all the necessary plumbing was installed years ago, there is no running water either in the kitchen or in the bathroom, for these buildings date from the Soviet era. The dry toilet is in the yard, and the hose lying nearby on the ground provides the water that the women and children of the thirty-five families collect each morning and carry to their apartments for their daily use.

The shore of the Aral Sea is today 62 miles away from Orasgul's apartment block. For her, it has only negative aspects: many children in the building have inflamed eyes and suffer from chronic bronchitis. The former island of Vozrozhdeniye can now be reached by walking across dry land. It was used by the Soviet Union to test biological weapons. Toxic waste was dumped into the sea, and since the two feeder rivers no longer carry water, the salt content is steadily increasing. At present, it is around two ounces per liter—in 1960 it was only one third of an ounce. All forms of life have died out.

Most of the aid organizations and the NGOs have been expelled from Uzbekistan. The questions being raised about the obvious problems had become too uncomfortable: How long will the corrupt system prevent reforms? When will revenues from cotton exports, gold, uranium, oil, and gas benefit the population at large? When will child labor be abolished? When will the health consequenes of ecological catastrophes be dealt with? The German enterprise GTZ, which promotes sustainable development, is still active and is planting saxaul trees in an effort to prevent the poisonous deposits in the Aralkum from being whipped up by the wind. Switzerland's federal agency SECO concentrates on the sustainable use of water, which it believes should be regulated through the introduction of a water price.

"Don't tear down your old house before you have a new one!"
This is President Karimov's message on a billboard campaign
calling for patience while waiting for prosperity and progress to
reach Uzbekistan. He is always surrounded by seemingly happy
young Uzbeks, who in reality dream of obtaining an American
green card. Loosely translated, *Uzbek* means "I am my own
master." When will this finally become a true statement?

The Amu Darya und Syr Darya rivers have not flowed
into the Aral Sea for a considerable time now. They
are pumped dry to irrigate the cotton fields. What is now
the contaminated Aralkum desert was once covered
by water. Mujnak

Alexander the Great knew the Amu Darya River
as the Oxus, and the Syr Darya as the Jaxartes. Tourists
traveling along the Silk Road between Buchara and
Chiwa can confirm that the Amu Darya still carries water
there.

The *mirob* has been an important figure for centuries, as he
is responsible for allotting the water. The water-intensive
system of traditional furrow irrigation has not been changed
in any way, as water does not cost anything and alternatives
such as drip irrigation are too expensive. Fergana Valley

The fish that the women at the market in Zizzach sell is no longer caught in the dying Aral Sea but in Aydarkul, the largest of the new salt lakes in Uzbekistan.

There is no running water in the apartments in this housing block in Mujnak. Around 35 families are dependent on the central water supply in the courtyard.

Смак
Источник жизни от самой природы

The cotton pickers are transported to the fields in the icy
cold of the early morning. Despite the high unemployment
rate, it is difficult for farmers to find enough pickers at
the right time. Near Pakhtakor

One hundred percent of the cotton harvest must be
delivered to the state. The "white gold" is Uzbekistan's
most important source of foreign currency.

A student protects herself from chemical traces and the
pointed leaves that can injure the fingertips while picking
cotton. She is supposed to pick 100 pounds a day.

The wages for all the pickers are six and a half cents
per pound. Thirty years ago, it was possible for a strong
man to harvest 220 pounds a day; today, the target
figure has been reduced to 130 pounds, as the yield has
decreased substantially through overuse of the fields.

As in the Soviet era, students and schoolchildren
aged fourteen and up are obliged to help harvest the
cotton, despite international criticism of this practice.
If possible, the children work close to where they
live; where this is not practical they sleep in schools
and gym halls.

Teachers also work in the fields during the harvest,
looking after the schoolchildren and students and keeping
records of the amounts picked.

Lagman, the Uzbek noodle soup, and *nan*, a round bread,
make up the staple diet.

Like everything that has to do with cotton, ginning is
also in the hands of the state, which has vegetable
oil pressed out of the cotton seeds. Cotton gin near Nukus,
Karakalpakstan.

Velvet materials made of colorfully patterned polyester
are fashionable among Uzbek women. They come
from China and are also worn there by Uighur women
who live in Xinjiang Province.

At the market in Zizzach, women illegally sell cottonseed
oil they have pressed themselves and which is often of inferior
quality.

Since independence in 1991, mosques, madrassas,
and caravansaries have been restored, partly with money
from UNESCO, for the growing number of tourists.
Samarkand

In some madrassas students can once again study
the Koran and, as here in Buchara, prepare themselves
for the end of Ramadan.

Lola dreams of getting an American green card. She lives
in Gagarin, one of the towns created amidst the endless
cotton fields on the former Hunger Steppe during the Soviet
era. Canteen of the gin in Gagarin.

Ürümqi
Aksu
CHINA
Peking
ShenXian
Jinan
Qingdao
Kunshan
Schanghai
Wuhan

MIÁN

"The culture of clothing: from Confucius by way of the Cultural Revolution to the 21st century"—the advertising slogan of fashion designer Carmen Zou is provocative.

"The culture of clothing: from Confucius by way of the Cultural Revolution to the 21st century" Carmen Zou's advertising slogan is provocative: the fashion designer deliberately flouts taboos, appearing naked on the Internet and taking Mao Tse-tung's fourth wife, Jiang Qing, as her inspiration for fashion and installations. "She was an artist. I want to show her soft, creative sides." In modern-day China, it seems, nothing is impossible. Carmen Zou clothes pop stars and actors in as many colors as possible. With a deliberate lack of value judgment, she randomly puts Madonna (both the religious figure and the US singer), Che Guevara, and Mao next to each other as decorative elements on her shirts and dresses. "I want to have fun, to be happy," she says. "Happy" is a word she often uses, also when speaking of Beijing, the city in which she lives and works: "Busy but happy." The fact that, as a member of the Gang of Four, Mao's wife sent thousands of men and women to their death or into exile in the 1960s and 70s degenerates into a cheap thrill for customers looking for a special Chinese fashion kick. Forty-three-year-old Carmen Zou's real name is Feng Ling. She grew up during the Cultural Revolution in a small village in southern China. Her mother was a teacher, her father an engineer, who returned a broken man after solitary imprisonment, forced confessions, and reeducation camp. "I saw him for the first time when I was five years old. The terror lay like a gray shroud over our family." Around the neck of this attractive business-woman—long black hair, fashionably narrow glasses—hangs a cross, and emblazoned across the blouse she designed herself are Mao slogans. "During my childhood there was very little color in China: communist red, Mao blue, police green, otherwise just gray, gray, and more gray." One glance at this artist's collection is enough to see that this gray era has now come to an end. Carmen Zou was one of the first to rent a loft on the disused factory site 798 in the northeast of Beijing. Other creative people and international art galleries followed, and now only very expensive cars park on the streets.

The cultivated romanticism of the rundown factory plays coquettishly with the Cultural Revolution and Mao's Great Leap Forward. The Ma family, farmers from the extreme west of Shandong Province, still remembers the reality of the old days, when door locks and tools were melted down to produce cast iron.

Large areas of the historic district in Shanghai are falling victim
to the booming economy and the rising real estate prices.
Factories and apartments are being moved from the city center
into industrial and residential parks, and enormous commuter
towns are being created on the outskirts of the city.

"Chairman Mao made a mistake there," muses the father, Taoxing. "In our village there was nothing to eat for two years." China's efforts in the 1960s to catapult itself from a state of backwardness to the forefront of the world's nations cost thirty million lives.

Jane, the youngest of the five children in the Ma family, translates the stories the old people tell us, while holding her little niece on her lap. "If your first child is not a boy, you can still have another try," she laughs. "My sister's first child was a boy but she was determined to have a second child. That meant she had to pay a fine, but she's worth 6,000 yuan (about 560 euros), don't you think?" The family is sitting together in the bedroom, the most formal room in the house. Neighbors drop by because of the visiting daughter, who studies textile engineering at university, despite her father's initial resistance: "He wanted my brother to study, but the teacher and my mother helped me." Secondary school was a particularly difficult time for Jane. The family had to borrow school fees and travel fares from relatives. "After my studies I'll pay it all back," she says, convinced that she will find a good job in booming China. For Jane, the era of the rural communes is a thing of the past, something that ended before she was born. The truth is that the decision made in 1983 to abolish the communes is one reason why Jane is able to study today. The land was distributed among the farmers' families: 1.3 *mu* per person. "We got six acres of land and can now cultivate whatever we want. Initially, we were allowed to keep or sell only the surplus above the official quotas, but today we're no longer obliged to hand over anything at all, as taxes for farmers have been abolished," recalls the father. "Next year I won't plant any more cotton; it's too much work for the two of us alone." He listens, impressed, as his wife tells him about a neighbor who has made enough money from the sale of peanuts to buy a computer. "We'll plant peanuts, too," he decides, "and even more poplars." Satisfied, and visibly proud of his daughter, the master of the house opens the bottle of schnapps that was bought for special occasions. The air is heavy with cigarette smoke, the floor covered with spat-out sunflower seeds. Jane fetches glasses: "I washed them myself," she laughs. "That way I know that they're really clean." There is neither criticism nor shame in her remark. It simply illustrates the distance between this graduate-to-be and her origins. There is a shortage of young people in the village, for most of them have moved away to cities to earn money as migrant workers. Jinhong, the second-oldest daughter in the family, used to work in a sewing workshop. She has been the proud owner of a clothes shop in the village for just three days. "You ought to see how busy it will be here during the three golden weeks," which is what the holiday season is called in China. CCTV 9, the only English-language station on Chinese television, is reporting a decision to create more holidays that people can choose individually. The Chinese are to be encouraged to spend money and stimulate the economy. "The boss was decent to us. We got paid every month," says Jinhong when asked how she was treated during her five years in a privately owned sewing workshop. "We worked eight hours a day, six days a week. I folded and packed 1,400 T-shirts a day." She is proud of herself and of her shop.

Not all migrant workers (there are said to be 200 million of them) are as lucky. Reports from Amnesty International tell of inhumane working conditions and wages that are kept back for up to a year or never paid at all because of company bankruptcies. Zongh, the only son in the Ma family, was also a migrant worker. Four years ago, a recruiter came by and promised work, food, and lodging in the city. "Here in the village we can survive, but that is about all." Today, he has a small grocery store and a car. "I did everything—worked on a building site, in a furniture factory, printed T-shirts." The shelves in his shop are stocked with instant soup, vacuum-packed sausages, and schnapps. His wife, Lijun, emerges from behind a curtain, their small daughter in her arms. A bed, a chest of drawers with a TV on it, and a big wedding photo of the couple in the style of Austria's Hapsburg Emperor Franz Joseph and his Bavarian wife, Sissi, make up the furnishings of the family's living area. The main street, on which both shops are situated, has been freshly tarred and is in prime condition. "There will be a lot of development over the next few years, and some of those who left will come back, build, and then settle down here." Like his parents, Zongh is content and has no fear of the future.

The journey to Qingdao, a major city in Shandong Province, leads past other villages, all of which look like Shenxian: gray-brown single-story courtyard houses are lined up beneath the teak trees and poplars which flank the highways and train tracks and provide greenery for the new residential and industrial parks in the cities. Behind them are fields surrounded by irrigation and drainage ditches, perfectly laid out and maintained. Line after line of greenhouses, endless rows of them, are covered with thick straw mats at night for protection against the cold. And chicken sheds are recognizable by the smoking chimneys of their heating systems, thanks to which the inhabitants are ready to be slaughtered only thirty days after hatching.

Spinning Mill No. 6 is one of Qingdao's state textile factories. "We place emphasis on high quality goods, and produce 120 different types of material and yarn, all made to order." Ju Yanjun, the chief engineer, is clearly pleased at our visit and uncomplainingly explains further details. "Our workers—there are 4,000 of them at the moment—are always developing new, modern blend fabrics which we then patent. We have a tradition of innovation." In the offices and factories hang photos of Mao Tse-tung with a worker whose invention streamlined the spinning process and is now used throughout China. As a reward, the Party financed her studies of textile technology. That young country girl, Hao Jianxin, is now a member of the government and a symbol of the values of the Maoist workers' and farmers' state. Chief engineer Ju Yanjun has been at Spinning Mill No. 6 for twenty-five years. The name alone implies state ownership; there are also beaches number one to six on the marvelous south coast of this city, which was founded by German colonialists. The factory building of the spinning mill was built in the 1930s by the Japanese in the *Jugendstil* style. This German architectural style has survived from the late nineteenth century and continues to dominate the old part of Qingdao. "I see no reason to go and work in a private factory. Production is growing and the orders books are full." He is referring here to the privatization of many state-owned businesses, a development already well under way along the coast. But changes are about to occur at Spinning Mill No. 6, too; it will soon move to a new industrial park, towards the north, about 30 miles outside the city. In ten years' time the industry is to be moved out, the old buildings demolished and replaced by new ones. The mounds of rubble in the neighborhood leave no doubt as to the credibility of this prognosis. As is the case throughout China, there is a rapidly growing real estate market here: prices in the inner city are up to 10,000 euros per square yard. "We'll move there, too," says Mr. Ju, taking a relaxed view. "The workers here are all permanent employees." There are no migrant workers here; the staff does not live in containers but in apartments belonging to the company. These apartments will also be demolished.

China's boom is restricted largely to the coastal region, where special economic zones were set up in 1979 under Deng Xiao-ping. Since 1992, the provincial capitals have also benefited from this concept. But outside these privileged regions, the level of the infrastructure sinks rapidly, with the majority of the population living at or below the poverty level. They are tied by the *hukou* system to their place of birth. Only there can they enjoy their rights as citizens, from medical care to education. It is almost impossible to live outside one's native district without a work contract. China's 17th Communist Party Conference was held in Beijing from the end of October to the beginning of November 2007. At the conference, Hu Jintao, China's President and Party General Secretary, outlined the most important goals in the further development of the "Chinese-style socialist market economy" over the next five years. There was talk of ecological sustainability and environmental protection, of the participation of the provinces and the rural population in the economic boom. Farmers are losing their land to the expanding areas of housing and industry. Workers in state businesses are losing their jobs as a result of closures. Many therefore decide to try their luck in the cities. Since they are not registered, they have no legal rights and are at the mercy of their employers.

Yet it is migrant workers of all people who have been building the new China; the new skylines, the stadiums for the Olympics, the new railway line for the high-speed train between Beijing and Shanghai, the irrigation canals, and the numerous shopping centers that stock everything that would be available elsewhere in the world—except for international newspapers. Censorship still weighs heavily on the press and television. There are black holes in the Internet, too, and over-critical journalists and poets end up in reeducation camps. But this reality is very distant to average Chinese citizens, endowed as they are with the blessings of the consumer goods industries. "There is no major opposition in the country. Why would there be?" A diplomatic representative in Shanghai explains that, as a surveillance state, China only rarely lashes out, and that it does not register the existence of a normal citizen until he or she has done something to cause a disturbance. "The Party tries to integrate the opposition, in the same way that the government includes businessmen and non-party members." The diplomat is fully aware that he is spied on. "Everyone, from the cleaning woman to the chauffeur, passes on information. My safe is the only secure place for documents."

For most migrant workers, though, surveillance is a non-issue. They are concerned with survival. At the day laborers' market in Qingdao, Zhao Lizhen has been trying to find work for five weeks. From five in the morning until sunset he holds up a cardboard sign offering his labor for construction, factory, or service work. "The market here is not completely legal. There are people who keep part of your wages when you get a job." But few employers go to the official agencies to look for workers, and there is a narrow range of jobs there which include board and lodging. Lizhen is twenty-six years old. The farmer's son gave up the chance of higher education in favor of his younger brother and is actually an artist, a calligrapher. He dreams of opening a library in his village. In his first job he earned 800 yuan (82 euros) a month, on top of food and a place to sleep. He then found work in a cafeteria. "I was there for half a year, and worked from five in the morning until eight in the evening, for only 700 yuan." In the nearby "hotel," he paid five yuan (about 52 cents) a night for a room shared with fourteen others. It had neither heating nor sanitary facilities, and it was so cold that everyone slept in their clothes. Lizhen stopped working in the cafeteria because it left him no time to concentrate on the most important things in his life: calligraphy and literature. He is now looking for short-term work because he plans to go home for New Year's, when there will be plenty of work for calligraphers in the village: inscriptions that bring good luck will have to be placed around house entrances, artfully inked with black paint on red strips of paper.

Mr. Li employs itinerant workers. He is the boss of the Meilian Garment Co. Ltd., a small sewing workshop in Kunshan, but he considering an alternative line of work, perhaps in computer hardware, because of increasing competition from countries like

Cambodia and Vietnam. This typical young, affluent Chinese citizen left university only three years ago. Since then he has managed a business with "only" 200 employees. "I didn't get any loans or subsidies from the state," he says when asked how he was able to finance it all. "My grandfather worked in the textile business, but during the Cultural Revolution he committed suicide." We stop asking questions, but the grandfather's money must have survived somewhere. The employees are, without exception, farmers from the provinces. They live in air-conditioned containers, and the cafeteria even has a television set. "It's hard to retain people. They stay for three months and then look for a new job." Larger firms try to counteract this labor tourism by organizing activities such as karaoke in the evening, and by providing senior staff with apartments they can keep if they stay with the firm for ten years. Mr. Li cannot compete with this. His seamstresses are paid by the piece, and earn between 93 and 130 euros per month. In the city he has to pick up his wife and their only son, whom they will send to America to study when he is fourteen. Mr. Li is proud of himself and of the opportunities he is able to offer his family. "My wife knows how to drive"—this is rare in China. "She's always going shopping and spends at least 5,000 yuan (about 512 euros) each time. Today, too, for sure."

On the train the next day, a commuter tries to engage us—the foreigners—in conversation, using the English she has learned from television. "We can't afford an apartment in Nanjing, even though we both work there," she says, describing her daily life. During the week her husband lives in an apartment that belongs to the factory, while she commutes between her home and workplace. "This is possible because I work for the railway administration." Her seven-year-old daughter is looked after by her sister. "I pay her for it, because our parents are too old." In China it is normal for children to grow up with their grandparents. The woman appreciates her state job, even though she does not earn much. It is true that there are many private employers, but they offer little security. "Things will be difficult for my daughter," she believes. "Competition for places in state universities is getting stronger and stronger." And so the parents have already begun saving about 9,300 euros for private school fees, as well as bribes for the teachers who select students for higher education.

We wish her good luck and further success with her language studies. "Unfortunately that's all over now," she says sadly. "The buildings around our apartment are now so high that I can't receive the English-language television station any longer!"

In the language of the Uighurs, the name *Aksu* means "white water," which sounds like a promise on the northern edge of the Tarim Basin. This is where the Gobi Desert meets the notorious Taklimakan region, which can be roughly translated as "He who enters will not emerge alive." The white water comes from the Tien Shan Mountains, creating climatic conditions that have turned Xinjiang Province into one of China's primary cotton-growing areas, in terms of quality as well as quantity. The fields are so large that entire brigades are still at work here, organized like the *shirkats* (collective farms) in Uzbekistan. It is not only the Uighurs here that remind one of that Central Asian country, but also the old towns that were founded on oases, as well as the agricultural conditions, for the cotton plantations depend on artificial irrigation. But unlike Uzbekistan, investments are being made here in water-saving technology. New canals are carefully sealed to prevent water seepage, and black hoses snake their way along the cotton plants, bringing water directly to the roots. This method, known as drip irrigation, is currently the best way to prevent loss of water through evaporation. In the fields, which are surrounded by poplars, cotton is rotated with corn, wheat, and vegetables, and between the rows of plants stand stone fruit trees, which are ideally suited to semi-arid climates.

It is often Han Chinese who seize the opportunity to build a life for themselves in this isolated and barren region, to which convicts were once banished. Xinjiang became part of the Middle Kingdom in the late 18th century, after a war against the khan of Kokand, who ruled in the Fergana Valley, in what is present-day Uzbekistan. The relationship of the Uighurs to the Chinese mother country is tense and the government in distant Beijing tries to keep the ethnic Muslim minority—which in Xinjiang Province in fact makes up the majority—under control by settling Han Chinese there. Yet the headscarves of the women, the square caps of the men, the mosques in the old part of town, and the bilingual signs leave little doubt about the self-confidence of the original inhabitants.

While strolling through modern Aksu, however, one sees no trace of an oriental Muslim atmosphere. The desert sky is reflected in the polished granite facades of the new buildings, which like to present themselves as a Chinese interpretation of Western Neoclassicism. Here, the nouveau riche who have profited from the economic boom—Han Chinese in the oil and cotton businesses—can find all the status symbols essential for displaying their prestigious position, as they can elsewhere in this land with its booming, Chinese-style socialist market economy. At midday, uniformed ladies from the municipal administration stand near the crosswalk traffic lights and, with their flags, try to prevent pedestrians from crossing the road when the light is red. Even during the worst turmoil and upheavals of the revolution, the color red continued to signify "Stop!" although devoted party comrades would have preferred that this significant color be used to mean "Go!"

View from Jinmao Tower in Shanghai's Pudong district.
Its height of 1,381 feet makes it one of the world's tallest
buildings.

Not all the former residents of the demolished districts
are able to find new housing. They are among the losers
of the economic miracle. Qingdao

China's 17th Communist Party Conference was held in
October 2007 and broadcast on large screens. Head
of State Hu Jintao explained to his fellow countrymen
and women the goals of the Chinese version of the
socialist market economy, which include improved living
conditions for the rural population and environmental
conservation. Ürümqi, Xinjiang Province

Zhao Lizhen, 26, is the son of a cotton farmer in Shandong
Province. He went without higher education, giving that
opportunity to his younger brother instead. He is a caligrapher
and dreams of opening a library in his village. But for now,
he looks for work at the day laborers' market in Qingdao.

Typical inner courtyard in the historic district of Qingdao,
which is shaped by German and Japanese influences.

The new commuter town Wuhan, where this apartment
is on offer, is about 25 miles outside the center. Those
interested in the apartments are transported by bus to view
the new buildings.

The advertising for the new housing developments is
directed at young, prosperous, middle-class couples,
a rapidly growing sector. The posters often show families
with more than one child and who are leading a Western
lifestyle. Kunshan

Ma Taoxiang, 64, a cotton farmer in Zhen, in the district
of Shenxian, has three children (right). The son and
the older daughter worked in the factories of Qingdao and
Beijing; now they each own a shop in the village.

Jane, the youngest daughter, is studying textile engineering
in Qingdao

The Party enables industrious workers and farmers to visit
China's cultural and tourist attractions, such as the Forbidden
City in Beijing and the Bund, the riverside promenade in
Shanghai.

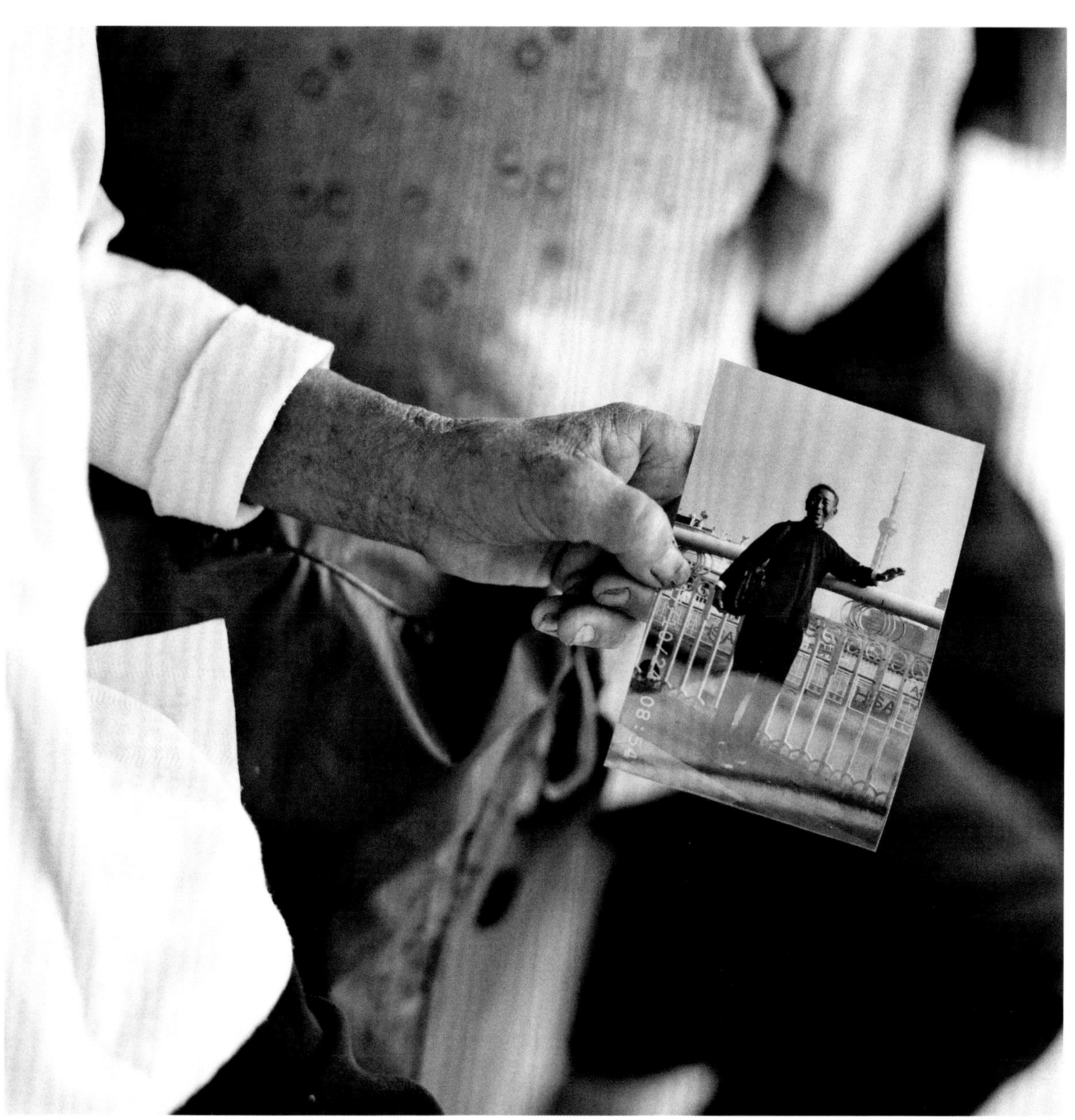

Construction workers and their campsites trail along
the irrigation canals being laid out in Xinjiang
Province, one of China's main cotton-growing regions.
In contrast to Uzbekistan, where the climate is very
similar to this desert area, water loss is minimized here
by properly sealing the channels. Near Aksu

The technology of the cotton cooperatives' machinery
does not always keep up with China's economic development.
Xinjiang Province

The cotton fields in Xinjiang Province are leased to
farmers, who are organized and regulated in cooperatives.
Workers from the poorer provinces come as pickers.
Their wages are so low that there is often nothing left
after the return journey home. Near Aksu

In Ürümqi, the capital of Xinjiang Province, the
Hong Kong-based Esquel Group operates a spinning
mill with 70,000 spindles. The machines come
from the Swiss company Rieter, which is experiencing
increasing pressure from Chinese and Japanese
competitors.

The state textile factory Wuhan Jiang Nan Enterprises
is soon to be partially privatized. The reform of the
Chinese economy began in 1979 with the opening of the
first special economic zones on the coast. In 1992,
Wuhan, along with all the other provincial capitals, was
made accessible to foreign investors.

Young country girls are trained to operate the looms.
Wuhan

"Labor tourism is widespread, with
  employees regularly changing their jobs
  for just slightly higher wages."

Despite the monotonous work, the textile factories
of China offer young women from the country
a welcome opportunity to achieve financial autonomy
and to escape the restrictive family relationships in
the villages. Qingdao

Attempts are made to retain employees—particularly
those of higher rank—by offering attractive leisure facilities
and financial assistance with buying a home.

The Yangshan deepwater port, the new free trade port
to the south of Shanghai, consists of a number of islands,
which are connected to the mainland by a bridge more
than 22 miles long. It is one of the main shipping centers
for raw cotton and textiles. Up to thirty container ships
can be loaded or unloaded at the same time—twenty million
containers annually.

Intertextile Fabrics in Shanghai's Expo Center became
the world's most important textile trade fair in 2007.

Fashion designer Carmen Zou, 43, was one of the first
to rent a studio loft on the disused factory site 798 in Beijing.
Today, the international art and gallery scene congregates
here. Carmen wants to be "happy" and to forget China's past
with her loud designs. Beijing

MALI
Djenné
Segou
Koulikoro
Bamako
Koutiala
Bougouni
Yanfolila
Sikasso
Balanfina

KOORI

"*Koori horon,* noble cotton, has changed my life." Beatrou Sidibé has no doubt about this.

"*Koori horon*, noble cotton, has changed my life." Beatrou Sidibé has no doubt about this. She was one of the first women in Mali allowed to plant organic cotton on her own land and on her own account—with the consent of her husband and the help of the Swiss aid organization Helvetas, which has been propagating its cultivation since 1998. Beatrou is about fifty and lives in Yanfolila, a small town in the southwest of the country, almost on the border with Guinea. The yard of her property is surrounded by mud walls; eight huts are positioned along this enclosure, round ones and square ones, crowned by pointed straw roofs. Her youngest grandson sleeps peacefully in a red plastic tureen, amid a buzz of chicken, goats, and other children. Under the shade of a roof in the center of the courtyard, we sit on low decorated wooden stools. Beatrou recalls the beginnings: "We were the second village to start producing organic cotton, in 2000. Twenty farmers, four of them women, two of whom soon gave up." She looks thoughfully at the red ground that is the same color as the mud plaster of her houses. "I had to raise 110 euros basic capital and received the same amount as a loan from the state cotton society CMDT"—something new for Mali, where women are for the most part excluded from the credit system.

The women get by by means of *tantine*, a kind of savings bank they organize themselves. Members of a group regularly pay in very small amounts, and the sum saved is then lent out in turns, either with or without interest. Aid organizations support this principle, which for many women is the only way to come by money.

Ten years ago, Beatrou saw her chance and took advantage of it. She bought an ox for plowing and a donkey and cart: the basis for working the ten acres of land on which she has since rotated cotton, sesame, corn and millet. This year's cotton harvest is in the storehouse, a small mud building decorated with geometric patterns, waiting to be transported away. During her career as an independent farmer, Beatrou has always been able to rely on the staff of Helvetas. The commitment by the Swiss has borne real fruit. Since those beginnings in 1998, the number of farmers growing organic cotton has risen to about 6,400, about 20 percent of them women. They combine forces in the female producers' association known as Mobiom, which has been entitled to bear

In the market in the center of Bamako, dressmakers
try to attract customers with photographs of dresses they
have made.

the coveted Fair Trade seal since 2005, enabling it to reach the appropriate customers. "Yes, my life has improved, thanks to *koori horon*," Beatrou repeats. "And I have cotton to thank for this, too," she adds, pointing proudly to a corrugated metal roof—the dream of African farmers, the visual nightmare of European visitors—covering the newest hut in the courtyard.

The courtyard is a flurry of activity, as daughters, daughters-in-law, and other wives pound corn with large wooden pestles to produce the meal that is to be served, as always, in a green plastic bowl on the ground. Tied to the back of almost every woman is a small child swaying along to the rhythm of the pounding. When the meal is ready, the entire family sits on the ground, using their hands to help themselves to food from the bowl. Beatrou Sidibé does not know exactly how many farmers in Yanfolila plant organic cotton. "I couldn't go to any meetings last year because my husband died," she murmurs indistinctly, for this is a private matter. Age, the number of one's children, and anything negative are also taboo topics in Mali. She was fortunate with her husband. He worked in the administation and supported her efforts to earn her own money. He left the land that she works not to his sons, but to her.

While we convince ourselves of Beatrou's success in Yanfolila, an official assessment of the organic cotton project is on the agenda, as Helvetas wishes to make Mobiom independent by 2013 at the latest. The experts gathered in Mali's capital, Bamako, have grounds for concern: too high a price for raw cotton, dependent local staff, and 80 percent reliance on foreign aid are the reality. The business plan offers no satisfactory solution to these problems. "The truth is that members of NGOS are not businesspeople and their way of thinking is not business-oriented enough," says Ton van der Krabben, one of the external experts. As if these problems were not enough, demand for organic cotton is not keeping pace with worldwide supply and many producers are left with their harvest. Beatrou knows nothing of all of this: "When I have sold my harvest I'll send my sons off to study." She is used to the payment practices of the Swiss and looks to the future with confidence, in contrast to many of her colleagues who are dependent on the bankrupt state cotton society CMDT.

The CMDT is a monopoly that no one in the cotton business can avoid. It administers all aspects of the industry: from the distribution of seed to the sale of the harvest, from the delivery of pesticides to loans for farmers. In a tradition dating back to the colonial era, the *Compagnie Malienne pour le Développement des Fibres Textiles* continues the work of its French predecessor—the only difference being that the "F" for France has been replaced by an "M" for Mali. In the best Francophone tradition it is centrally organized and a joint venture in French and Malian hands. It was decided to privatize it in the summer of 2008. After long resisting the pressure from the World Bank and the International Monetary Fund (IMF), Mali's parliament had to give President Amadou Toumani Toure, or ATT for short, its approval on this matter. A search then began for an investor to direct the fortunes of the three million people involved in the production of Malian cotton. As of 2008, this investor was yet to be found. In 2006, with 600,000 tons of raw cotton, Mali was the largest of the West African cotton producers, who for their part were number three worldwide. This year, production has sunk by two-thirds to around 200,000 tons, as increasing numbers of farmers are deciding to change over to food crops, which yield a greater and, above all, more secure income.

Noel Diarra is one of them. Wearing a full-length white boubou and Muslim head covering, he is standing, at the end of a day's work, in his courtyard in the savanna near Koutiala, a region of Mali that was once a top cotton-producing area. Termite mounds and baobab trees form the landscape and recall the look of the *Lord of the Rings* films—the castles of fantasy characters and trees that fight for justice. From a portable radio hanging in Noel's tree we can hear one of the many local stations reporting about protests by workers who used to work for the CMDT cotton gins (machines that separate the cotton fiber from its seed) and oil mills in the city. More and more of them are being let go and, along with their families, they face an uncertain future. Noel has drawn his own conclusions. "I got my pay for last year's harvest only two weeks ago," he says in a resigned tone of voice. "I'm giving cotton up." He harvested the two and a half acres of land with the help of his wife and oldest children, and the cotton lies neatly arranged in the yard. "It's good quality," he assures us, while pressing a few of the white bolls into our hands.

Like the farmers, the factory workers in Koutiala are also waiting for a reaction from Bamako. "I really can't tell you when we'll be able to collect the harvest from the villages," says Amadou Sow, the director, when asked about the abandoned collection centers distributed throughout the bush. Their walls are gradually crumbling into dust and the tracks leading there are becoming overgrown with thorny scrub. "Bamako doesn't send any gasoline for trucks, lubricant for the machines, or steel bands for the export bales." Noel did not want to wait any longer and decided to sell his harvest illegally to dealers waiting on the border to Niger. "They pay us less than the CMDT, but at least they pay immediately." He has planted cotton for forty years, without artificial irrigation, without fertilizer, and without machines. In fact, he would be able to compete with the big farmers in the USA and Brazil, who cannot produce without high input costs, but the national and international cocktail of corruption and lobbying is forcing him to abandon cotton. At least for the present.

It may sound like the name of a rock band, but "The Cotton Four" actually refers to Mali, Burkina Faso, Chad, and Benin, which have been resisting American and European subvention policies since 2003. The four came to the aid of Brazil after it lodged a complaint a year earlier, and which at that time was a smaller producer than the West Africans but nevertheless ready and willing to take on the Americans—not only in meat and soybean production, but also in cotton. The arbitration court of the WTO ruled in favor of the plaintiffs, on the grounds that the nature and extent of agricultural subsidies made fair competition between all cotton producers impossible. "Those who receive them," they argued, "are completely independent of market and other production risks. Guaranteed prices lead to overproduction, which lowers the world price, at times even below the low production costs of the African and Indian farmers, making it impossible for them to sell their harvest at a profit." The current condition of the CMDT, which at times has been quite successful since the colonial era ended in 1960, is a result of these circumstances. Despite internal corruption it made a profit, which at times accounted for about half of Mali's foreign exchange revenue. It paid the farmers guaranteed fixed prices, invested in the infrastructure of the villages, cotton gins, and oil mills and, as the officials of this large agency were able to divert enough money for themselves, everyone was happy. This system, which suited everyone, began to teeter when the CMDT paid the farmers more for the cotton than it got on the world markets and could no longer balance the losses. The remaining alternative for the farmers is to plant rice or sesame. Many workers from the gins and oil mills are going to neighboring countries to look for work. From there they will send money to their families. Or perhaps not.

The Millennium Development Goals of the OECD countries include halving the number of those who have to live on less than one US dollar a day by the year 2015. The overall aim is to strengthen the position of women in developing and emerging countries, who are forbidden to play an active role in social and economic life because of religious beliefs or other traditions. Despite this, they are the ones who usually make a decisive contribution to the support of their family. In this context Beatrou Sidibé and her story seem to constitute a successful experiment. We meet her again on October 15, which the UN has declared International Day of Rural Women. Mobiom has invited new and old members to exchange views in the town of Bougouni, located in Mali's most productive cotton-growing area, the Sikasso region. An animated discussion soon gets under way. "How can we persuade the *dougou-tigui* to give arable land to us as well?" This is the main problem that concerns the fifty or so women who have traveled here from Kayes Province, in the west of the country. The *dougou-tigui* is the head of the village, who generally comes from the family that was the first to settle in the area. Together with the village elders he makes all the decisions that affect village life: this is the tribal tradition. History is passed on orally, as are the facts about the arable land, which is allotted according to need—to the men! No purchase price exists outside the cities, nor is there a land registry office. "We have to share two and a half acres of land with twenty women!" one of the visitors calls out to the group. While doing so she deftly moves her newborn baby from her back to her breast. The other women murmur their agreement, and with increasing courage the woman continues: "We carry the dung to the fields on our heads as we don't have money for donkey carts of our own." This is an example of extreme poverty, even for Mali, where women carry everything imaginable on their heads. In the general confusion of voices the female staff member from Helvetas stands up: "We are aware of this problem, you just have to be patient! Take Grande Seur as an example!" Everyone falls silent and all eyes are turned to Beatrou Sidibé, who moves shyly out of the protection of the masses. She is wearing a wraparound skirt, a blouse and matching foulard, the piece of cloth tied to form a large ribbon that covers the head of every married woman. Then, as recognition for her work over the last ten years, she accepts a check for more than 45 euros, a large sum that represents the monthly salary of a teacher.

The supply chain of cotton in Mali is traditionally relatively short, as the French colonial rulers exported most of it. There are only two textile factories that weave the material that Mali women use for their clothing, printed with mementos of festivities, with advertising for private Christian schools, or with the portrait of much-loved President ATT. The gins and oil mills that meet the country's requirements for cottonseed oil are of greater importance. One of these is the Hikoma oil and soap factory in Koulikoro, but hanging over this extensive factory site, which was privatized back in 2005, is a melancholy silence, much like the one that hangs over the cotton gins in Koutiala. "There are no cottonseeds to press. So far the CMDT has not delivered any," Awa Diakte comments drily. She is the president of a cooperative to which about one hundred women belong. Her face is hidden behind a widow's veil, but this does not prevent her from providing accurate information about the production processes in the factory. "The oil has to be refined three times before it is suitable for use as cooking oil. We collect what is left and turn it into soap. We've been doing this for more than twenty years." The tarry leftovers from the refining process used to flow into the Niger, but for some time now the director of the factory has shown a willingness to cooperate and allows this raw material, which is of value to the women, to be collected in rusty barrels. One of the women is standing on three large stones, between which some of the sparse wood of the savanna is going up in flames. Another woman is stirring the blubbering contents with a large wooden spoon, while others beat and knock the cooled mass, forming it into grayish balls about the size of a grapefruit. The soap is sold in this form at all the markets in the country.

"Business is going well, 14 cents per piece," she says with an air of satisfaction. "No one here can afford Omo." In a corner of the yard there are two barrels full of the raw material. "That's all we have left. If more cottonseed for crushing doesn't arrive soon, we'll have nothing more to do."

There are many international aid organizations working in Mali, one of the poorest countries in the world. They delegate tasks to smaller national NGOs with the aim of integrating local workers into the implementation of the programs. This creates an important job market for local graduates. Due to structural adjustments insisted upon by the WTO and the World Bank, there are fewer and fewer priviliged jobs available in the corrupt state administration, which is the traditional employer of the educated upper class. Now employed by the NGOs instead, they form a real caste and live, for the most part, in the relative comfort of Bamako. It is primarily their luxury jeeps, along with the many buses in the city, that whirl up the dust on the streets. They are specialists in writing grant applications to the international donor community, which generously distributes money. Everybody knows that only a part of this money reaches those whose situation the OECD countries want to improve. Indeed, critics of development aid argue that it merely helps to institutionalize clientelism, which has a long tradition in Mali, just as it does in other former colonies.

Through family connections Madame Kij Kadiatou Touré also belongs to this caste, but she does not have a four-wheel-drive jeep. Instead, every week she travels hundreds of miles through the bush on her moped. "This is my job. At the moment I look after thirteen villages," she tells us cheerfully, for she is successful in her work. For three years she has been campaigning among the population against female circumcision, a practice that still affects about 90 percent of the country's women and girls. Madame Touré used to work in the state health service in the area of hygiene and AIDS prevention, but went five years without receiving a salary. After moving to CAEB, a national NGO, the contacts that she had built up in her previous job helped her in tackling this difficult taboo. "The entire village of Sido has abandoned the practice and I hope that Farabakoro will follow suit," she says on the journey to this distant location in the middle of nowhere. There, the *féticheur* draws magic symbols in the sand while a family expectantly waits for him to proclaim the best time for the circumcision of their little daughter. The woman who is to perform the circumcision arrives, carries out her macabre work, and once again all convene, this time at the magician's, as there have been complications. Medicinal herbs are sought and found, but they do not help. The child is bleeding to death and only the doctor at the hospital can save her. At least twenty villagers are wholeheartedly involved in this play, with which Farabakoro is taking part in a competition set up by Madame Touré as part of her work. Fiction and reality blur after the final act in which the participants, with astonishing openness, discuss the consequences of circumcision for sexual intercourse and childbirth. Amid peals of luaghter from the audience, the new bride flees from her husband's bed back to her mother, something that often happens in real life, too, as Madame Touré remarks in a whisper. While the relatives in the play discuss giving back the bride price, the bride herself is preparing for her main scene, the most important part of the event, in which she delivers her plea, to the village elders gathered around her, against the complete or partial removal of the outer genitalia. "I am also circumcised," she says, "just like my sister and two of her daughters!" She bravely introduces her own experience, explaining why she has spared her own daughter this practice and is nevertheless convinced that she is a good girl and will make a good wife. For this is the worry of many parents. Tribal myths mingle with the interpretations of the imams, "many of whom cannot even read the Koran, for nowhere does it call for the circumcision of women." This was confirmed in 2005 by the highest Islamic dignitaries at the Cairo Conference, but who in the villages south of the Sahelian zone cares about this? Mali signed the 2005 Maputo Protocol for the rights of African women. Under Article Five, female circumcision is defined as a crime but there are no legal consequences. The intellectual and political elite officially distance themselves from this practice. "Yet they still have their girls circumcised. Not with rusty razor blades, but in the hospital, under general anesthetic, generally during the first week of life." The discussion at Farabakoro's meeting place is in full swing: "Yes, I also had problems giving birth," a young mother dares to admit. Her remark provokes general laughter, the typical reaction to delicate topics. And then comes the straw poll: Who is in favor of abolishing circumcision? The hands of both village elders, one a traditionalist, one from the administration, go up. Is this reason enough for optimism on the part of Madame Touré and the girls of Farabakoro?

There is little cause for optimism in Yanfolila. "A theater group from Burkina Faso that presented a play on this topic was pelted with stones," recounts Mamadou Kameradine, a hunter, *féticheur*, and farmer, in a low voice. His mother, a stout matronly woman fanning herself in a corner of the yard, carries out circumcisions herself: on girls from her own family and, for a fee, on others too. After the operation, bandages keep the girl's legs pressed together until the bleeding stops and the healing begins. And what if something goes wrong, we ask, looking at the hunter's amulets hanging on his suit. "Then that means there is something negative involved and it must be removed," he answers, this time in a normal voice as this is his area of competence. Mamadou regularly goes hunting for warthogs and gazelles in the bush. He sells the leftover meat, along with the skulls, teeth, and horns that are used by traditional healers to bleed their patients. He does not plant cotton. "Too much poison," he says matter-of-factly. "Not good for the women." Most of them are pregnant or nursing their babies and traditionally do not help with cultivation. His only contact with organic cotton has been as an actor, through Helvetas, which wanted to motivate new farmers to take part in this program by means of a play. But he knows Beatrou Sidibé, her story, and, above all, her new corrugated metal roof. "I'll think about it," he says when asked whether he would allow his three wives to follow her example. He lowers his voice as he says this, his gaze directed at the matron seated in the corner of the yard.

Women farmers are not given loans by the banks.
NGOs propagate the *tantine*, a system of micro-
credits from women for women, which has a tradition
in a number of areas of Africa. Bougouni

On October 15, the International Day of Rural Women,
the women cotton farmers meet in Bougouni at the invitation
of the Swiss aid organization Helvetas to exchange their
views and experiences. The village is in the district of Sikasso,
Mali's most productive cotton-growing area.

On account of the high levels of harmful pollutants,
women stay clear of fields where conventional
cotton is grown. The risk for unborn babies and small
children is simply too great. Balanfina, Sikasso

"The truth is that members of NGOs
are not businesspeople and their
way of thinking is not business-oriented
enough."

The state television station is also present and
interviews a number of women about their experiences
with the production of organic cotton. Balanfina

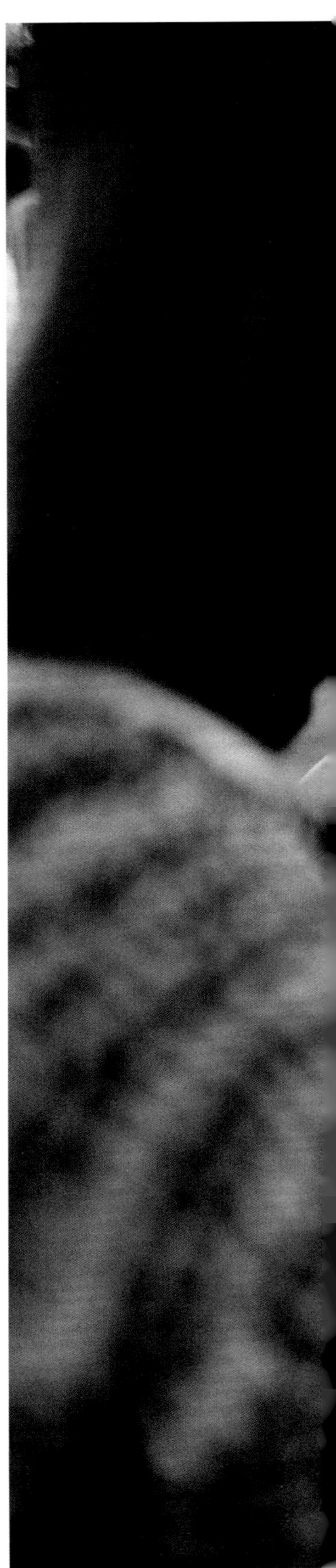

Very small amounts are paid in regularly. The sums
saved are then paid out in turn to the different members
of the group. Often the women use the money for their
children's education, or save to buy an electric corn mill.

In 2000, Beatrou Sidibé became one of the first women
in Mali to begin cultivating organic cotton, with the help
of Helvetas. Yanfolila

Madame Kij Kadiatou Touré works for CAEB, a national
NGO. In the remote village of Farabakoro, she attempts
to persuade the inhabitants to abolish the practice of female
circumcision. Around 90 percent of women in Mali are
affected by this practice. Near Bougouni

The inhabitants of Farabakoro stage a play as part
of a competition initiated by Madame Touré. Even
the woman who performs circumcisions in the village
plays a role in this consciousness-raising program.
The story of a circumcised girl is very close to reality.
Near Bougouni

President Amadou Toumani Touré, known by all as ATT,
at the inauguration of the new blacktop road from Bougouni
to Yanfolila. It was built by a Chinese firm. Bougouni

Political, religious, and social manifestos of all kinds are
found on the wraparound skirts produced by the Comatex
textile factory in Segou. Bougouni

My ♥ lovely
CHER PAPA NOUS NE T'OUBLIERONS JAMAIS
26-12-1935 - 05-02-2008

This young boy has to earn his living in the fields of his better-off neighbors. The Fair Trade seal stipulates that children must not be taken out of school to pick cotton. Yanfolila

This family in Koutiala, Mali's cotton center, owns seven and a half acres of land. They pick around 660 pounds of cotton daily, and for two days a further twenty day laborers are employed. They work for 80 cents per day plus their midday meal.

Women dye imported damask under the most primitive
of conditions. In a lengthy process, wax is then beaten
into the colored fabric. This produces *bazin*, an expensive
material used to make clothes for important occasions.
Bamako

The market in Djenné is held every Monday. It is also
a tourist magnet,, as this is the only day on which they can
visit the famous Mosque of Djenné, the largest mud-brick
building in the world.

The storefronts of Mali are decorated with fantastical
paintings. This tailor and dressmaker also sells charcoal.
Sikasso

178

The women in a cooperative produce soap out of the
waste products from the Hikoma oil mill. Their future
is uncertain, as is that of the entire cotton industry
in Mali which suffers from the insolvency of the state
cotton monopolist CMDT. Koulikoro

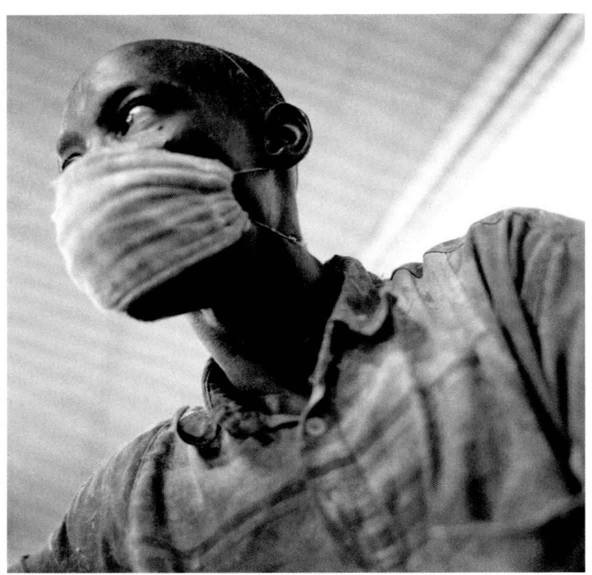

The formerly state-owned Malian-Chinese company
Comatex is the larger of the two textile factories in
Mali. It is now in private Chinese hands and employs
1,400 workers. The higher-ranking employees are
Chinese, who stay an average of two years in Mali.
Segou

Mamadou Kameradine is a hunter, *féticheur*, and farmer.
He also took part as an actor in a theater campaign that Helvetas
started to develop awareness about organic cotton. Yanfolila

There are 1,323 pounds of conventional cotton in the storehouse
of this family in N'Togonasso, near Koutiala. When the CMDT
pays for it, it will bring in 200 euros.

The Suore del Santo Natale di Torino have been working
in Koutiala since 1993. Sister Franca, the head of the
religious order here, complains that aid money arriving
in Mali often fails to reach those in need because of
corruption and bureaucracy. Many malnourished children
reach the center too late because their mothers do not
get permission to leave the village, where they are needed
to work. Koutiala

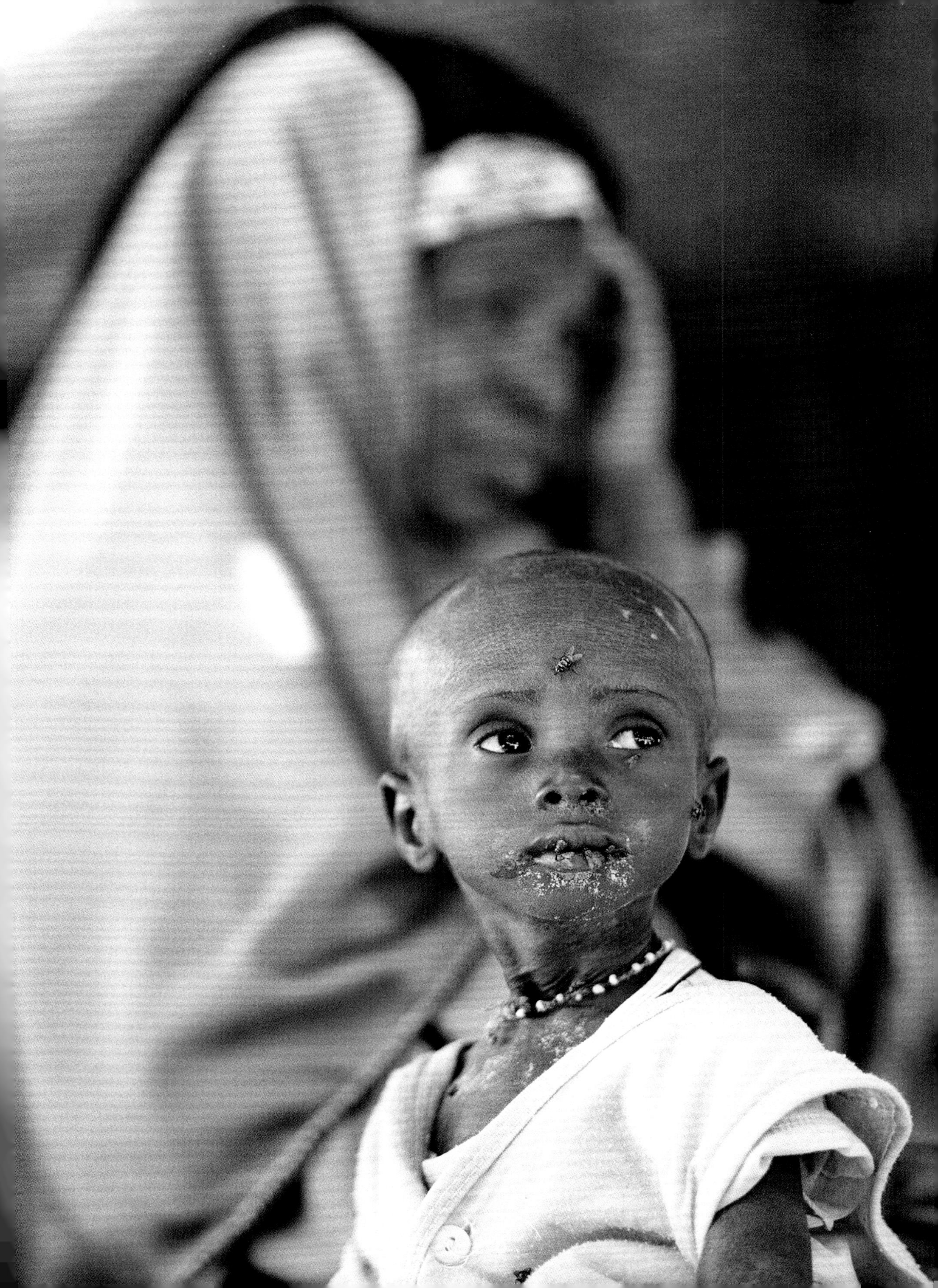

Miss Mawa Malaika is a singer. For a record cover she
has herself photographed wearing a cotton dress with *bogola*,
the traditional mud painting on fabric. Bamako

Itaquatiara
Manaus
Santarem
Maguari
Itaituba
BRAZIL
Novo Progresso
Cuiabá
Primavera do Leste
Rondonopolis
Brasi

ALGODÃO

"Have no fear, everything will be
all right." Perhaps August Prochnow
sought to calm his wife, Luise,
with these words when they began
their uncertain journey from Hamburg
to Porto Alegre in southern Brazil
in the steerage of the *Freiheit* in 1874.

"Have no fear, everything will be all right." Perhaps August Prochnow sought to calm his wife, Luise, with these words when they began their uncertain journey from Hamburg to Porto Alegre in southern Brazil in 1874. The couple from Hoffstädt, in the Pomeranian region Deutsch Krone, faced ten days at sea, traveling in the steerage of the *Freiheit*. After that, a better life was to begin in the New World, one in which recession, hunger, and persecution would be things of the past. A photograph shows the Prochnows looking earnestly into the camera, probably well aware of what awaited them: wilderness and hard pioneering work, a life that had been in the blood of the inhabitants of Pomerania for centuries. Their gaze is also proud and determined, for they are bringing money with them, enough to buy land in Rio Grande do Sul. Other Germans already live in this area, and they will be welcomed and given encouragement in the Lutheran evangelical community, where the language and customs of their native land are cultivated—down to the present day.

"I could fill a water pail, and more, with all the tears I've shed," says Iria Prochnow more than a century later. She has just made *chimarrão*, the maté tea of the gauchos, which is being passed around the group in wooden mugs under the shade of the mango trees that her husband, Oldemar, planted ten years ago. Oldemar and their youngest son, Raffael, are listening to the text from the New Testament that Iria is reading aloud, which she does every day, as the lady missionary from Germany comes to the Amazon rain forest only once a month; to Novo Progresso, somewhere along the BR-163 highway between Santarém and Cuiabà. "You must never look back, but always bravely ahead, otherwise nothing will work out," says Iria, summarizing the creed that once drove—and still drives—the pioneers in places with names like *Esperança* (Hope), *Novo Horizonte* (New Horizon), or *Novo Progresso* (New Progress), even though the latter may seem very far away indeed. The town was built in 1993 on a square grid with two-story buildings that contain hotels and shops for farmers, cowboys, and the occasional gold digger. The dark red sand track that runs through the state of Pará widens in the urban area to four lanes with a wide median. This urban gesture, reminiscent of the USA, seems even more inappropriate in Novo Progresso than it does elsewhere in Brazil, for during

the rainy season both street and grassy median are transformed into a slippery mud track that brings every form of traffic to a standstill.

Oldemar Prochnow arrived here twenty years ago, on the roof of a truck, as there were no buses here back then. Further south, in the state of Mato Grosso, he had risked, and lost, everything. Continuous rain had washed the soybean harvest, the farm, the harvester, and the tractor into the hands of creditors—everything that he and his wife had built up over the years. While telling us this, Oldemar looks at the leg that went lame in his youth, forcing him into a life as a tailor. "My brother was an apprentice tailor but he drowned," he recalls, and Oldemar therefore took the place of his drowned brother. After those heavy downpours the Prochnows had no idea how their life was to go on. They already had three of their four childen and were once again earning a living from sewing. Oldemar suffered bouts of depression "because I didn't want to work as a tailor any longer, but on the land, like my parents."

And then one day it came along, that typical Brazilian opportunity: further north, in the forests of the state of Pará, the state settlement authority, Ingra, was giving land away again. Oldemar looks proudly at his farmhouse. It is roughly built from planks which bear the marks of the chain saw, a tool that he has used almost every day for the last twenty years. "You could get as much land as you wanted, a mile and a quarter off the BR-163 down as far as the Rio Curuà, that's where the Indian reservation starts," he says, recalling the early days when he and six friends combed the impenetrable woods in their search for the best grazing land. Five of those friends—strangely enough it was the ones who had money—soon gave up; they could not take life in the jungle and did not believe in the success of the undertaking. Only Ivo, the Italian neighbor, and Oldemar remained, both of them without any money but with a desperate determination to build a new life.

By 2000 the time had come: Iria and young Raffael came to Rurica, the name of the Prochnows' *fazenda*. The husband and wife had not seen each other for two years. The marriage had almost broken up because of the distance, as well as the setbacks that Oldemar regularly had to accept. "He came to Rondonopolis and I was barely able to recognize him." Iria is fifty-nine years old, very thin, almost skinny, slightly stooped. The features of this woman, who, as she herself will tell you, likes to laugh and talks too much, grow hard when she recalls how she took her husband to the hospital after one of his numerous attacks of malaria—as many as seventy, it would seem. Oldemar plays this down: "No, malaria won't kill, but the liver damage might, later on, if you don't watch out." He has lost a number of friends this way over the years.

Oldemar chose his 4,000 acres of land well: flat, gently undulating grazing land for the 400 cattle that he currently owns, a river suitable for fish farming, a field for beans and manioc. From the only hill on his land the view extends a full 360 degrees across the jungle, untouched and majestic. "The forest will never vanish, no matter what they say about us!" He is referring to international environmentalists, Brazil's former Environment Minister Marina Silva, and IBAMA, the "forest police" environmental agency which has prohibited any felling of timber this year. The farmers are allowed to clear only 20 percent of their land; for the Prochnows this means only 200 acres more before they reach their limit—and they need this land, as their herd of cattle is constantly increasing. In Novo Progresso alone there are one million registered cattle. The animals have to survive journeys of several hours to the nearest slaughterhouse, in transporters that get bogged down in mud during the rainy season or surrounded by gusts of burning red sand in summer. Building slaughterhouses is pointless unless you have paved roads, for it is impossible to schedule the journeys of the refrigerated transport vehicles. A look inside a local supermarket reveals few vegetables and almost no dairy products. The Prochnows store their meat in a freezer belonging to friends who live on the BR-163, as that is the only place that has electricity. Rurica is nine miles off the road, along a clearing that the men cut through the forest. Whenever he wanted to cook for himself or make a phone call home, Oldemar would walk a total of 24 miles: nine miles through the forest, three along the road, and then the same distance back again. To earn money for tools and materials, he also worked for his neighbors, who came to Pará thirty years ago and own the *fazenda*s along the main road. "I'm at an age now when men need garlic pills," says Oldemar, adding without no obvious sign of regret that at the age of sixty-nine he can no longer handle such a workload. Not that he has to, for in front of his house stands a tractor, a car, and a generator, which every evening pumps water out of the well located directly under the kitchen. He dug it himself, 39 feet deep. How did he know that there was water there? "I didn't know for sure—but I wanted to have the well here in the kitchen," is his terse reply. And then, like every evening, he turns on *Beleza Pura,* a *telenovela* that all of Brazil finds spellbinding. In the meantime, Iria has been preparing the evening meal. There is always rice and beans, then meat and fish, and the few vegetables that she can grow between the rainy and the dry seasons. "You'll find life in 'Brazil' easier," she says, referring to our imminent departure. "They have blacktop there. You'll see that things are better there than they are here with us!" She means the part of Brazil that has a better infrastructure. This view is shared by the neighbors who gather for a religious service the next day—the lady missionary has arrived, contrary to all expectations. The entire congregation comes come from the south of Brazil and is descended from German or Italian immigrants. "We know how to deal with this country, we want to get ahead," which is why they are the ones doing the pioneering in Pará.

The other locals in Novo Progresso are mostly *caboclos*, descendants of the original Indian inhabitants and white immigrants. They used to work in the sawmills, which were once the foundation of all the town's hopes for progress. The sawmills are standing idle— the ban on felling trees is making itself felt. "The people from the IBAMA ought to be killed," says Ivo, in a somewhat unchristian spirit, "just like the rats, the snakes, and the Indians." Nobody here has a good word for the Indians: they're said to be corrupt and to do things on their reservations that they should be punished for. There is talk of illegal timber transports and gold prospecting with chemicals that pollute the rivers. "On many reservations they allow that, for a share in the profits." Then it is time for the evangelical congregation to begin its service and for us to journey on to Cuiabá.

Late in the afternoon, Novo Progresso disappears behind us in a cloud of dust kicked up by the hooves of 1,600 cattle being driven from one pasture to the next. Our bus gets stuck in the mud only three times. After that, we change vehicles and find ourselves on a different road surface, which can only mean that we have arrived in "Brazil."

"Sustainabilty? In the Amazon rain forest?" Dr. Philip Fearnside considers this for a moment, then says, "That would require leaving it completely in peace," which is clearly such a utopian idea that for a moment stillness descends upon the small office, full of filing cabinets and stacks of files piled all the way up to the ceiling that look as though they are ready to collapse at any moment. Dr. Fearnside, a well-known American researcher and argumentative admonisher regarding the tropical rain forest, has spent the past thirty years in the muggy heat of Manaus. This jungle city, with a population of well over a million, used to be the glorious center of the rubber barons. Today it is a tax haven for those in the microelectronics business. On the wall hangs a newspaper clipping with a caricature of him: mid-fifties, tall and gangling, the lower half of his face hidden behind a thick moustache. In an article entitled "Polemica," he criticizes the planned extension of the BR-319 highway from Manaus to Porto Velho on the Bolivian border. "At the moment, you can travel this route only by airplane or boat, but once the blacktop arrives that will mean an end for the forest." Although he is a state official at the INPA *(Instituto Nacional de Pesquisas da Amazônia,* or National Institute for Amazonian Research), Dr. Fearnside is now clearly annoyed about the government's PAC Program, an infrastructure program for the north of Brazil which aims to encourage economic growth without taking ecology into consideration at all. The development of the Transamazonica roadway and the connection to the neighboring countries in the north and the west are part of this program, as are new power stations and settlement schemes. "Once a drivable road is in place, legal and illegal settlers very soon move in about 31 miles to the right and left of that road, fell and market the timber, and begin to open up pasture land," says Dr. Fearnside, briefly summarizing a development that is depressingly regular. Under Environment Minister Marina Silva, who has since resigned out of frustration, initial efforts were made to save the the forest, partly in response to pressure from the international community. "This involvement does achieve something," says Dr. Fearnside reflectively. For example, the PPG7

Program that produced 400 local, non-state organizations. He himself was a consultant to the program and is convinced that the original inhabitants can provide the best protection for the forest. "Brazil is a corrupt country, a banana republic, and if illegal loggers enter the forest, what do you do? Call the police?" He looks at us defiantly. And even if the police check things out: the unpaved roads cannot be used during the rainy season, there is no telephone, and cell phones have no reception. And the pressure from the overpopulated south and the poor north-eastern area of Brazil is enormous. "A railway line brings the ore extracted from one of the largest iron mines in the world from Carajas to the port of São Luís. Passengers are allowed to travel with the train only once a week, and each time around one hundred families come—with all their belongings! And this has been happening for years now." In this region nothing of the forest has survived. *Caboclos* are the original inhabitants of Maguari, one of three villages in the Floresta Nacional do Tapajós nature conservation area, which owes its creation to the PG7 Program. Bebé rents us a room in his new little house, which the Ingra settlement authority has placed beside his traditional hut of wood and palm leaves. Similar houses are also found beside each neighboring hut. Posts for a new power line are positioned along the crudely cleared strip on the mud track, which during the rainy season provides the sole means of access to the park. "Light for All" is a government slogan. Bebé works with tourists, whom he takes to see trees that are 600 years old and up to 197 feet tall, while other families live on state welfare, known as *Bolsa Familia* (Family Grant), around 35 euros a month. A community building financed by the German development bank KfW (Kreditanstalt für Wiederaufbau) stands empty; factories were to be built for rubber and wood products but nobody works here.

"This year we are planting 23,500 acres of cotton," explains Eurides Baumgart during a tour of Petrovina Sementes. The Prochnows' son-in-law has been bookkeeper on this *fazenda* for twenty-five years. It forms part of the 200,000-acre agricultural empire of the Augustin family. "But fertilizer and diesel have become too expensive, so next year we'll probably concentrate more on soybean, as there are already enough nutrients in the earth for that." The *cerrado*, the steppe landscape of central

Brazil, can be made and kept arable for large monocultures only with the input of large quantities of chemicals. In the 1970s, the military government sold the apparently worthless land in the state of Mato Grosso at a low price to the first prospective buyers. They use it for their herds of cattle, leaving degraded ground behind, and move further and further north, into the Pará rain forest, where Oldemar Prochnow and his neighbors are opening up new pasture land. Cotton has been produced in Mato Grosso since the 1990s, so successfully that Brazil has moved up to fifth place among world producers. This is possible thanks to chemical cocktails, but only as long as they are affordable and generate profits. The fleet of machines at Petrovina Sementes looks like an agricultural trade fair: about one hundred tractors, countless special machines for the production of soybean, and twelve John Deere cotton pickers, each of them worth 210,000 euros. At a respectful distance is a landing strip for the four "airships." Like his parents-in-law, Eurides Baumgart also speaks the Pomeranian dialect of his ancestors. The skulls marking the pesticide store put the idyllic Sunday afternoon atmosphere into perspective, for the crop-spraying planes are among the most important machines. "Nine to fourteen sprayings are normal," Eurides reports. "When the pests get out of control we fly up to seventeen times." And they are getting out of control: in the shape of worms, fungi, and in the form of the bicuda, the much-feared beetle, they penetrate the monocultures, prompting a need for ever-new, ever-stronger pesticide mixtures. "The boss is in Brasilia, trying to improve our situation here," says Eurides, apologizing for the absence of Carlos Augustin. He is lobbying for Brazil's cotton farmers, who get almost no subsidies and who for years, in collaboration with West African cotton producers, have been taking action against the subsidy policies of the Americans and the Europeans. Topics such as the construction of a railway line from Rondonopolis to the coast are also being discussed, along with the release of genetically modified varieties, and the implementation of state-guaranteed minimum purchase prices.

Life on the farm begins on Monday morning at around six o'clock. Some of the 400 workers live here: the singles in hostels, the families in small, single-family houses. Breakfast is served in the canteen: rolls, salted margarine, and strongly sweetened coffee—also for the seasonal workers who work on the farm from January to May. There are 270 of them this year. They have been hired not to harvest the crop, but to eradicate the weeds; despite all the agrochemicals used, people are still needed to remove the persistent weeds between the rows of cotton plants that would otherwise hinder the harvesters.

Ronaldo is one of them. He comes from the Maranhão "hunger region" in the northeast: "I've been coming here for the last few years," he tells us on the bus that takes the workers out to the fields, "and this time, too, I'll be staying until August to help with the stripping!" His father also works on the *fazenda*, while a brother and the women look after the small farm at home: "We plant manioc, vegetables, and we have our own goats!" The young farmer's features are marked by homesickness. A wide-brimmed hat protects him from the sun, a mask and a sheet of plastic wrapped around the body from dust and chemicals, and leather shin guards offer protection from snake bites. He has to clear eight rows of weeds in one hour. Piecework. "The workers get about 240 euros a month, as well as food, lodging, and medical care, if necessary," says Euridis, who knows all about what things cost. The family in Maranhão can live until the following year with the money that the two men take home.

"The good thing about President Lula is that he has not criminalized the MST (*Movimento dos Trabalhadores Rurais Sem Terra*), even though the land reform movement has come to a standstill," explains Padre Jose, our "entry card" to the Accampamento Quilombo near Varjao, one of the provisional tent towns in which the occupation of a *fazenda* is being prepared. One meets families here, like the Ronaldos, who despite all their efforts have not managed to keep the small farms of their ancestors and who now live on the city periphery. About one hundred huts made of plastic sheets, lined up one after the other, seem almost idyllic in the shade of the trees, along a bubbling river in which children are swimming and catching fish. "For many, this represents an end to moving from one place to another, and an end to their uncertainty." Padre Jose knows the backgrounds of the people here and is clearly loved by all. *"Tudo Bom"* is heard from all around, and thumbs are pointed towards heaven.

Brazil's Landless Workers' Movement has existed since the 1970s and is based on a promise anchored in the constitution: "Agricultural land must meet its social responsibilities"—an elastic phrase that everyone, except the big landowners, interprets as meaning that it should be used to produce foodstuffs, preferably for the often still hungry population of Brazil. "But this is what we are doing," reply the meat producers, who make most of their profits with exports to China. "Each cow needs five acres of land!" The members of the movement see this differently, for "five acres are enough for a family to lead an independent and dignified life."

In the state of Pará, settlers are allowed to clear up to
20 percent of their land to create pastures for herds of cattle.
A figure of five acres per animal is generally used. Charred
Brazil nut trees, which by law must be left standing, are
like a silent admonishment as they face the bare areas cleared
of trees that have been converted into planks in numerous
sawmills.

Despite international protests, the felling of the rain
forest continues. Environment Minister Marina Silva, who
battled to save the forest, resigned her position in May
2009, as it was not possible for her to achieve her goals in
the face of opposition from the legal and illegal timber
and meat lobbies.

Indian zebus are apparently ideally suited to the wet,
hot climate of Pará. In the course of the year the gauchos
drive the animals from pasture to pasture on exhausting
marches that can last days.

In the state of Mato Grosso, herds of cattle have been
degrading the soil of the *cerrado* since the 1970s. The
big landowners sell their *fazendas* there and come to Pará,
where there is still inexpensive, unused land, as here,
near Novo Progresso.

Manaus, a city in the middle of the jungle with a population
of more than one million, was the center of the rubber barons.
Tax incentives are now intended to attract microelectronics
firms to the city—a double-edged sword, as the creation of the
necessary infrastructure will further endanger the ecological
balance.

XIII° FESTIVAL DO BOI VIVO
BANDA REGIONAIS: DIA 03/04
TORNEIO e BINGO - PRÊMIOS: 12 B
REALIAZAÇÃO: WALTER   APOIO
MIGUEL e CANHOTO - PREFEITURA-IRANO

According to the latest calculations, the Amazon is the longest river in the world. Many settlements along its banks can be reached only by boat. The arrival of the steamboat, which brings not only travelers but also goods of all kinds, is the high point of the week.

During the rainy season travel is often impossible on
the BR-163 from Itaituba to Cuiabá. The people living nearby
are waiting for the road to be paved, as that will allow the
delivery of dairy products and vegetables from the south, as
well as electricity and slaughterhouses, which will save
the cattle from being transported for several days under highly
distressful conditions.

The Transamazonica and the BR-163 meet in Itaituba.
These are two of the main traffic arteries through the Brazilian
jungle. Here, ranchers and gold diggers buy provisions,
conduct their official business with the authorities, or visit
the doctor.

A new *fazenda* is being created. First, an area is cleared
to build the farmhouse. Together with the water
cistern and generator, this forms the heart of the complex.
Then the pastures for the cattle follow. Until 2008 this
was legal in the state of Pará. Then all felling of trees was
halted until further notice. Novo Progresso

Twenty years ago, Oldemar Prochnow, who is of
German origin, came to Pará, where the state settlement
authority Ingra was releasing new areas of forest.
"You could get as much land as you wanted," recalls
Oldemar, who is now sixty. He took 4,000 acres.
Novo Progresso

For the first twelve years Oldemar was alone in the forest,
and caught malaria many times. Since 2000, his wife,
Iria, and son Raffael have also lived in Rurica, the name
of the Prochnows' *fazenda*.

It is generally the descendants of German and Italian
immigrants who clear the forest to create new *fazendas*.
Their wives are proud of being able to cope with the hard
conditions of life there. There has now been a generator
in Rurica for three years. It runs for two hours each evening
and supplies electricity for the water pump, the deep
freeze, the iron, and the TV set.

216

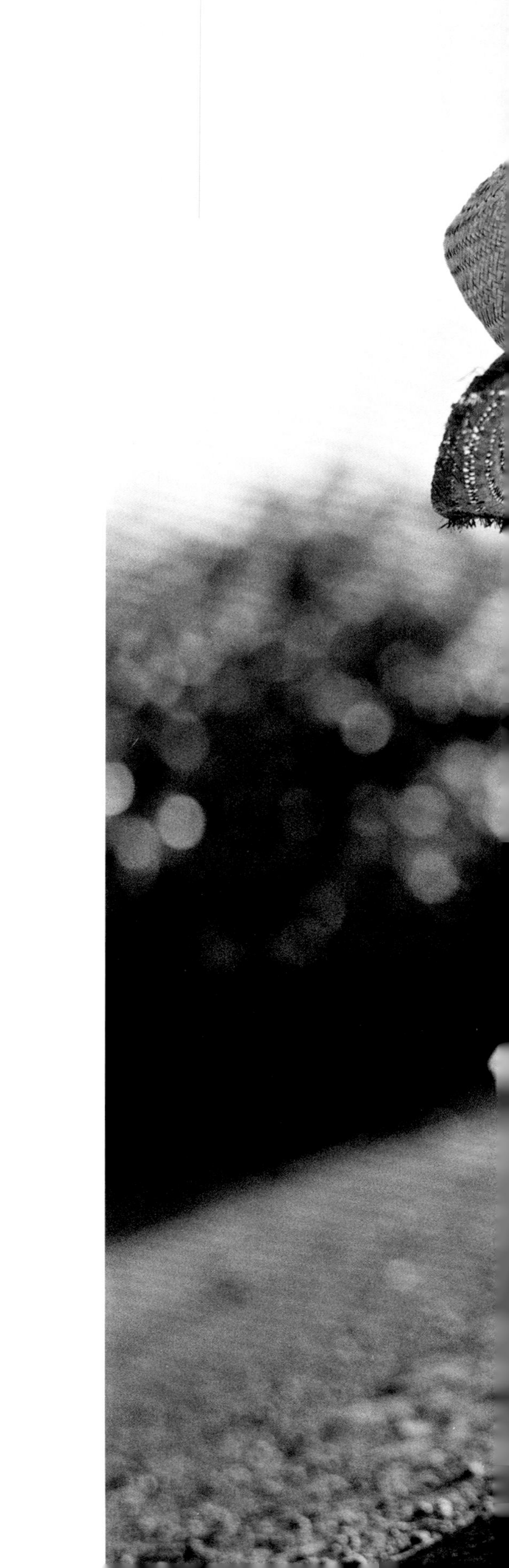

The *fazenda* Petrovina Sementes is in the state of Mato Grosso. In the 1970s the military government sold the apparently worthless land of the *cerrado* to interested persons, such as the Augustin family, which acquired 200,000 acres as grazing land for their cattle. The vegetation of the savanna was entirely eaten up. All that remained was degraded soil, which since the 1990s has been used to grow cotton and soybeans, with the help of large amounts of fertilizer.

Four hundred workers are employed throughout the year on Petrovina Sementes, one of the largest *fazendas* in the state. This year their numbers are being strengthened by 270 seasonal workers, as weeds must be removed by hand before the harvest, despite the fleet of agricultural machines and the widespread use of chemicals. Company buses transport the workers to the cotton fields, which consist of 24,000 acres this year. Near Rondonopolis

The men protect themselves from chemicals and the early
morning dew with sheets of plastic. Leather shin guards ward
off snake bites.

The farm's own aircraft spray the cotton up to seventeen
times with pesticides and, if necessary, with growth inhibitors,
as the harvesting machines can access only plants with
a height of up to around four feet. Near Rondonopolis, Mato
Grosso

"Nine to fourteen sprayings are normal.
When the pests get out of control we fly up
to seventeen times."

"Just another few years and then I'll have saved enough
money to find a wife in my home state of Paraná and raise
a family there. No woman would come here of her own
volition," says Cesar, an agricultural technician who works for
the big landowner Paolo Machado. Primavera do Leste

Paolo Machado comes from a Portuguese family. In the
1970s his father bought land near Primavera do Leste,
and the son followed suit twenty years later. He now cultivates
15,000 acres of cotton on both farms. He produces about
one million liters of biodiesel each year from the cottonseeds
left over after stripping the fibers in the farm's own gin.
This is just enough to run his fleet of agricultural machines.

The raw cotton is pressed directly in the fields into blocks
weighing eleven tons and is later taken to the gin by special
trucks. Primavera do Leste

Primavera do Leste celebrates its 22nd birthday.
Like many towns in Mato Grosso, it is hardly older
than the young residents from the south of the
country who find good career opportunities here.

According to the Brazilian constitution, agricultural land must
satisfy certain social requirements. The MST, or *Movimento
dos Trabalhadores Rurais Sem Terra,* organizes the occupation
and takeover of *fazendas* that ignore this requirement in a
particularly crass way. Those involved sometimes spend years
in *accampamenti,* provisional tent camps in which they are
prepared for this undertaking. Near Brasilia

The period spent waiting for land is used for various
training courses, in some cases also to teach people how
to read and write. Near Rondonopolis

Those registered as looking for land with the settlement authority
Ingra benefit from financial support—for many, this is reason enough
to opt for life in an *accampamento*. Near Brasilia

USA
New York
Washington
Amarillo
Memphis
Lubbock
El Paso
Fort Worth

COTTON

"None of us here could survive
without subsidies, but it's no different
in Europe."

The scent of freshly made coffee and newly printed newspapers spreads through the offices of the Meadow Farmers Co-Op, where, like every morning, the cotton farmers are meeting to exchange news. The faces under the wide-brimmed hats are marked by the stress of recent weeks; storms have raged across the flat countryside, endangering the first sprouts of the cotton plants. Last night Keith Harrison lost what is called a circle of cotton, one of the typical circular fields. The others cannot yet assess the situation and are engaged in battling for their seedlings with sand fighters. "Without them farming here would be impossible," explains Dan Jackson, the manager of the gin, where the cotton seed is separated from the fiber. He is solidly built, in his early thirties, and grew up as the son of a gin manager. "Yes ma'am," he seems almost to salute. "The sandstorms come in early summer every year, that's normal here."

Throughout the world young cotton plants are exposed to stress, generally caused by pests or water shortages. The Texas High Plains is the largest continuous cotton-growing area in the world. In this semi-arid climate, fine sand is brought to the earth's surface after heavy rainfalls and then swept through the young plants at great speed by the strong wind. The sand seems to be suspended in the air, filtering the sunlight and bathing the fields in a dull yellowish light. The tractors pulling sand fighter trailers, which are replowing the earth between the rows of plants, are barely recognizable. "This brings the heavy, wet layers of earth to the surface, where they defy the wind, at least for a few days," Dan explains, shouting to be heard over the wind. He waves at a barely visible worker from Connor Farm who, with an almost artistic assurance, is breaking up the ground in forty furrows simultaneously, like his colleagues in the other fields, for at the moment there is nothing else they can do.

Later in the breakfast room that is sheltered from the wind, he tells the stories of his farmers, often the descendants of the first white settlers who wrested their land from the Indians in the nineteenth century. The Connors, for example, the largest landowners in the area. "Don only moved three times in his life, really ma'am, always only one square further," like a chess figure on the mile grid that subdivides the town and the county of Lubbock. His family is among the few that still lives in a farmhouse

Independence Day—July 4, 2008, in Lubbock, Texas.
The parade ends on the campus of Texas Tech University,
which specializes in research into cotton. Lubbock is
America's cotton capital and the center of the High Plains,
the largest continuous cotton-growing area in the world.

amidst the fields. Many of their former neighbors travel the forty miles from town every day, where their wives work and the children have a better education. Abandoned, half-decayed timber houses along the farm roads illustrate this trend that has not spared the small town of Meadow: there is not a shop or a gas station to be seen and the local bar is long gone. This makes the windowless chamber of the cotton gin all the more important in the lives of the farmers.

Bagels and doughnuts are served in our honor with the morning coffee, but the farmers look distrustfully at the visitors from Europe. They are aware of the bad image they have had since 2003 at the very latest: back then Brazil, backed by Mali, Burkina Faso, Chad, and Benin, took a case to the WTO arbitration court against the subventions that the USA gives to its cotton farmers. The decision was made in the plaintiffs' favor; the court ruled that such subsidies made fair competition between all cotton producers impossible, and recommended that they be abolished by 2013 at the latest. Since that time discussions have taken place in a number of Doha Rounds without any concrete results about how this should be done, accompanied by controversial and often polemical reporting in the international press.

"Will you be objective or do you work for Oxfam?" is therefore the first question we have to answer at the beginning of our visit to the PCCA, the Plains Cotton Cooperative Association. In addition to marketing cotton—between three and four percent of the worldwide production—this organization, one of the largest in the world, lobbies politicians in Washington for the continuation of the disputed subventions for its members. It was only with the help of the association that the farmers in Meadow opened their doors to us, but now they eagerly tell us about their life in southwest Texas. "In fact, they wanted to continue traveling further west, but the oxen that pulled the covered wagons collapsed. Otherwise no one would have stayed here," Don Connor jokes, telling us why his ancestors from Ireland, Scotland, Germany, and Italy settled precisely here and exposed themselves to the rigors of the climate, the heat, and the sandstorms, described so hauntingly by John Steinbeck in his novel *The Grapes of Wrath*. Don took over 6,000 acres of land and the machines from his father and grandfather, and is expanding further.

He also owns shares in the gin that separates the cotton fibers from the seed and in the oil mill in Lubbock. This enterprise brings him about 15 percent of his annual income. "French fries taste best if they are fried in cottonseed oil." Most Americans are convinced of this fact, and their consumption of fast food and snacks helps increase Don's profits, as does the purchase of nail polish and X-ray film. He is over sixty and has therefore reached the average age of American cotton farmers, who number around 25,000. "The 'O' in the Irish surname O'Connor got lost somewhere during the last few generations, but we also have Indian blood in the family," he tells us, proud of this connection to the earth he farms. But all the same: "I want my son to have a different job, something with a steady income." This is an astonishing statement, given that the farmers receive a state-guaranteed income, direct income payments that were recently confirmed again in the 2008 Farm Bill.

"None of us here could survive without subsidies, but it's no different in Europe," says Keith after the silence that follows Don's statement, and he is right, as percentage-wise, subsidies for cotton growers in Spain and Greece are even higher than those in the USA. At thirty-five, Keith is by far the youngest of the farmers. He moved to Meadow ten years ago because it is his wife's hometown. Reason enough for the older farmers to energetically support the greenhorn. Today, he is respected by all as he is on the right path to realizing the American dream: "1,250 acres of my own land, no longer just leased the way I used to have it!" An acre of dry land costs about 224 euros. Where there is enough water for artificial irrigation, the price quickly rises to double this figure. He already owns several tractors and special machines for cotton, including a harvesting machine that costs 245,000 euros; 350 cattle graze the land where cotton is not planted. And all of this although it is said that planting cotton no longer makes economic sense, although the income is uncertain, and although the prices of gasoline and agricultural chemicals are rising continuously.

A closely woven net of insurance, direct and indirect payments to cover running costs, loans at favorable interest rates, and export aids means that Keith can take the loss of a circle of cotton relatively easily, whereas Indian cotton farmers can be driven to commit suicide by a failed harvest. More than anything else, it is the state-guaranteed minimum price of around seventy-five US cents per pound of raw cotton that constitutes the difference between him and his colleagues in the rest of the cotton-growing world. This is around 17 cents above the world market price of 35 cents per pound, which just covers production costs, also for the Africans, Brazilians, Chinese, and Uzbeks who grow cotton. Surplus production from 2007, which is still waiting for buyers in the warehouse in Lubbock, lowers the world market price and makes the struggle for survival of cotton farmers in the rest of the world more difficult. Their contact to a profitable textile chain generally ends with the sale of the raw cotton; for Keith, Don, and the others it starts with the ownership of the gin, the oil mill in Lubbock, and the denim factory in Littlefield, one of the last textile factories in Texas. Despite all their difficulties, from an international perspective their position is very good. "Recent years brought record harvests, ma'am!" Dan, the gin manager, tells us delightedly. In addition to good weather and the sand fighters, this is also thanks to the researchers from Monsanto and Bayer, whose genetically modified crop varieties are grown on more than 70 percent of American fields. The companies charge heavily for the decades of research and development work. "The seed used to come in sacks, now we pay for each seed individually," he says, attempting a joke about the high price of "Round Up" or "Fibermax." "The technology charge is higher than the price of the seed, but it's worth it."

In the Texas High Plains the water required for record harvests comes from a huge underground water table lake with the somewhat difficult name "Ogallala Aquifer," which extends from Nebraska to under the fields of Meadow. The farmers get the water for free, because in addition to land rights, and from time to time mineral and wind rights, they also have water rights, which they take full advantage of. "And what if there is no more water?" This question is one that concerns not just us but also the researchers at Texas Tech University. Tectonic movements have caused the southern part of the lake, which was created at the same time as the Rocky Mountains, to separate from the rest. Rainwater can hardly keep it full. "Then we'll plant dry cotton again," Dan Connor says with a coy smile. "Until the 1950s nothing else was available." But he hopes that it will not come to this, as fields that are not irrigated produce about one third less cotton. Like most of the farmers, he owns computer-controlled pivots, sprinkler systems that can even be activated by telephone, and he has experimented with drip irrigation by laying pipes underground in a number of his fields. "I can irrigate so much more cotton with the same amount of water," he reports with satisfaction. This increased production has little to do with ecological sustainability or the development of the cotton price—and nothing at all with saving the Ogallala Aquifer. Dan places his hopes in the scientists who are working feverishly on the development of varieties of cotton that save on water. In the greenhouses of Texas Tech University, plants with especially large leaves are being raised. As they cast more shadow, they prevent the earth from drying out. Other scientists are trying out the opposite and are attempting to reduce the amount of water that evaporates by raising plants with particularly small leaves. The ancestors of all these plants come from Uzbekistan, where the Aral Sea is drying up because its water is being used to irrigate cotton. American development aid organizations are propagating the introduction there of a water price to save the sea and with it the hydrological balance of Central Asia. Scientists at Texas Tech University say that if the same amount of water continues to be taken from Ogallala Aquifer to ensure record harvests, then its water will run short in about twenty-five years' time.

On July 4 the small cotton plants are out of danger. The farmers and their families can relax, and they travel to Lubbock to celebrate Independence Day. Everywhere fathers are to be seen wearing big hats and boots made of ostrich, crocodile, or rattlesnake skin, accompanied by sons wearing a mini-version of the same outfit. The parade passes through the center of the town that will celebrate its 100th birthday next year. From the town hall it continues down Broadway, which is lined by stately houses and an impressive number of churches of different denominations. The goal is the campus of Texas Tech University, a large complex of neo-Gothic and neo-Renaissance style buildings in a park-like setting. Representative of the various military branches lead the parade. In the middle are the recruits, young, some of them women, and at the end march the veterans. Almost everyone holds one hand to their heart, while the other hand waves the American flag. There are no sand fighters to be seen, but there is a police car looking for young recruits. The army recruiting office has closed, but many of the churches are open. The members put together care packets for the sons on the front. In Texas, patriotism begins with breakfast waffles in the shape of the Lone Star State and ends in the evening on the way home with a pavement design in the same form.

"I was seventeen when I joined the Marine Corps. I was in the Pacific and apart from the war all I knew was my parents' farm." Eighty-three-year-old Isaak G. Holmes sits in his photo studio on Avenue Q at the corner of Broadway in the old part of Lubbock. Many of the commercial premises nearby are empty. As in other downtown areas which seem to be turning into ghost towns, the shops have moved to shopping malls along the highways. "After the war the Army gave us training and I wanted to to take photographs," he says, recalling the beginnings of his career as a photographer, which he started with a poor GI school and poor equipment, "junk equipment" as he calls it. His career also started with photographs of visitors to the Cotton Club, where alcohol was served, which led to his expulsion from his church community. "I looked for a new church—after all, we have plenty of them here," he says, laughing at the bigotry of his fellow citizens, for even today Lubbock is the "wettest of the dry districts." As no photography studio wanted to employ him, he set up his own, called "Darkroom," with which he earned barely enough to pay the weekly food bills. "To make money, I took on every kind of job, and I also dismantled the guns from the B-17 bombers at the airport." This is where the fate of I. G. Holmes begins to intertwine with that of cotton. He transferred from the photography school to a pilot school and since then has photographed everything that has to do with cotton, preferably from the air. "I got my first commission in 1947 from the Plains Co-operative Oil Mill." Although he was not yet officially permitted to fly, Holmes took the job, flying with one hand and photographing with the other, "real easy!" he says, with skillful understatement. By mistake he photographed not the oil mill, but a nearby cotton gin instead, which showed a record harvest: 300 bales of pressed cotton fibers (each bale weighing 500 pounds) were stored in the courtyard, five times more than the standard harvest before the war. "Suddenly everyone wanted aerial views," Holmes chuckles, recalling the proud farmers' wish to document their success in black and white. For more than sixty years he has photographed the gins of the High Plains, the oil mills and the warehouses, the farms and the development of the town of Lubbock, through all its highs and lows. There were a great deal of lows, for example, in 1968 when it first became clear that the water of the Ogallala Aquifer was running out. Windmills that once pumped water for humans and animals are still the only landmarks in wide expanses of Texas, which did not get electricity until after World War II. "There were plenty of motors for the water pumps back then, left over from the Army," Holmes says, explaining the sudden growth in the number of artificially irrigated fields, which in 2007 delivered an unbelievable 117,000 bales of cotton compared with 350 cotton bales during the post-war years. Old photos show Mexican handpickers. They were legally allowed to work on the harvest during a period known as the Bracero Program, which lasted until the 1960s. "That was a good move on the part of the government," says Holmes, "useful for both the Mexicans and us." Despite widespread mechanization, the need for seasonal workers grows massively during the harvest and ginning periods, but the work is hard and it is still mostly Mexicans that are interested in the four to 5.50-euro-an-hour jobs. Many work illegally on the cotton fields near El Paso. Security fences and walls along the Rio Grande, the green water border between the USA and Mexico, are an attempt to prevent this.

Isaak G. Holmes is proud of his work and has stayed on the ball all his life, also in technical terms. When color photography came along he needed thousand-watt bulbs for the reflectors that had to be placed close to his subjects. "I could see my clients growing redder and redder! I could only take a maximum of six shots, otherwise they would have caught fire!" His anecdotes are as varied as his photos. He has been taking digital photos for a long time now, and has been working with the pilot of a small plane that has a special opening in the floor for the camera. The results are photographic paintings, reminiscent of the work of Paul Klee: the squares of the street grid overlaid with the circles of the pivot sprinklers that travel like gigantic compasses over the fields, producing green or white circles, depending on the season. Holmes responds indignantly to a question about retirement: "I'll go on, who knows what's going to come for us in

Lubbock," which at the moment is the uncontested capital of American cotton. Two hundred thousand people live here, about half of them from and with cotton.

Dr. Magdy Alabady at the Functional Genomics Center of Texas Tech University is one of them. At present he is involved mostly with the *Kirkii gossiboidis*, an ancestor of the present-day common varieties of cotton. It has only thirteen chromosomes, making it highly suitable for examinations. "The genome will be decoded in a year at the latest," Alabady is convinced. The young Egyptian is part of Thea Wilson's team. Wherever this world-renowned grower of cotton plants is, money for research is there, too. She recently came to Lubbock, attracted by the Bayer Company, which is now focusing its cotton research around this scientist. "If you know only the makeup of the genes, it's as if you owned all the books in the national library without knowing what is in them!" Dr. Alabady tries to explain the complex context of his work. "We attempt to understand the task of every single gene before we intervene." Experts call this the "functional genomics approach." "Housewife genes" is the name he gives to those responsible for the basic function of the cells. More interesting are the other ones, for example, those that direct the production of cellulose. Here, the issue is the quantity and quality of the cotton. "It's only when we exactly understand the way the plant functions that we will be able to modify it genetically to create an organism that is completely functional and can therefore reproduce itself." The standard genetically-manipulated varieties today cannot reproduce themselves. Every year, expensive new seed has to be bought, a significant cost factor for the farmers from Meadow, and one of the reasons for the suicides of some Indian cotton farmers.

In the USA, researchers and farmers work hand in hand; the machines on Don Connor's farm are equipped with GPS that can identify which fields the harvested cotton comes from. The pressed bales that come to the state quality control and certification center have bar codes with details about the owner and origins, allowing conclusions to be drawn about growth conditions at any time. The demand in the spinning mills of India and China is constantly growing, and the machinery of the US cotton industry is responding to this demand. Traditionally, short-fiber cotton was grown in the High Plains of Texas, eminently suitable for providing material to the denim factories. Today, however, the farmers of Meadow harvest cotton of a quality that previously grew only in California. "But nowhere in the world will you find anything like Egyptian cotton," enthuses Dr. Alabady with true patriotism. He lives in the USA only because the conditions for research work are among the best in the world. Then it is time for lunch. On the way to "Bless Your Heart," a restaurant directly beside the heart clinic, he tells us about a Turkish colleague who recently moved to Lausanne, as "the food is a lot better there." Whether he means this ironically or not remains unclear. While eating a low-calorie salad and drinking mineral water, we watch the line of cars at the dispensary of the clinic pharmacy. Nobody has to get out of the car—and perhaps that is for the best, as the drivers have their hands full of fast food fried in cottonseed oil, paid for with dollar bills containing 70 percent cotton!

NYMEX
ClearPort
NYMEX
NEW YORK MERCANTILE EXCHANGE
NYMEX
miNY

In contrast to oil, which still changes owners on the
NYMEX, the New York Mercantile Exchange, all dealings
in cotton are handled electronically.

Violent storms that can even develop into tornadoes
dominate the weather in early summer. Lubbock

Many small settlements such as Old Glory resemble
ghost towns. The inhabitants have all moved to
larger towns; the farmland is leased or owned by big
landowners. Texas

The farmers use sand fighters to battle against the destructive
force of the sandstorms. After thundershowers, the sand in
the earth comes to the surface and is whipped up by the wind.
Flying grains of sand can mean the end of the tender cotton
plants that have just sprouted. This is the greatest danger they
are exposed to in Texas. Meadow near Lubbock

"Yes ma'am, the sandstorms
   come in early summer every year,
   that's normal here."

The farmers meet at the gin in Meadow every day
to discuss the situation. They are members of
the Plains Cotton Cooperative Association (PCCA),
which lobbies in Washington for the continuation
of the subsidies laid down in the Farm Bill.

Don Connor is descended from Irish pioneers who
settled on the High Plains around 1870. He is proud of the
fact that he has never moved further than a mile from
Meadow, where he was born. The parents of his Mexican
workers came to Texas in the 1960s in the course of the
Bracero Program. Meadow

The denim factory in Littlefield is one of the last textile
factories to survive in Texas. It is owned by the cotton
farmers, as is the Pyco Industry Inc. oil mill in Lubbock,
whose products are found in many foodstuffs. French
fries that have been fried in cottonseed oil taste best; this
is an open secret in America.

It is becoming more and more difficult for Mexicans who cross
the border to work legally in the USA. For hundreds of miles,
the Texas Border Wall, with its fences and watchtowers, flanks the
Rio Grande, which here forms the border. Field near El Paso

In June 2008 the surplus production from the 2007 season is still
waiting for buyers, some of it outdoors, as the warehouses are full.

Cliff Bingham and his wife with some of their eleven children, who
are homeschooled. The family has been planting organic cotton
for years, as the price is good and demand is growing. Nevertheless,
Cliff is leaving each of his children two and a half acres of organi-
cally cultivated grapevines, as he does not believe there is a future for
American cotton without agricultural subsidies. Near Meadow

Photographer Isaak G. Holmes, 83, has documented
the cotton-related activities of the High Plains for sixty years,
mostly from the air. Lubbock

Texas cotton farmers are not only to be found on sand
fighters. In their leisure time they also ride bulls. Rodeo near
Amarillo

The geneticist Dr. Magdy Alabady comes from Egypt,
a cotton-producing country. He views the conditions for
research in the USA as among the best in the world.
He is working on the team of Professor Thea Wilson on
deciphering the genetic code of cotton, using what is
known as the functional genomics approach. Texas Tech
University, Lubbock

Dr. Jane Dever grows cotton for Texas Tech University.
One of the varieties she raises conventionally produces
huge leaves that are intended to prevent the ground
from drying out. She works with varieties from Uzbekistan
that need less water. Texas Tech University, Lubbock

In the Standardization and Engineering Branch of the
US Department of Agriculture's Cotton Program, quality
standards for cotton are laid down which are recognized
throughout the world. Memphis, Tennessee

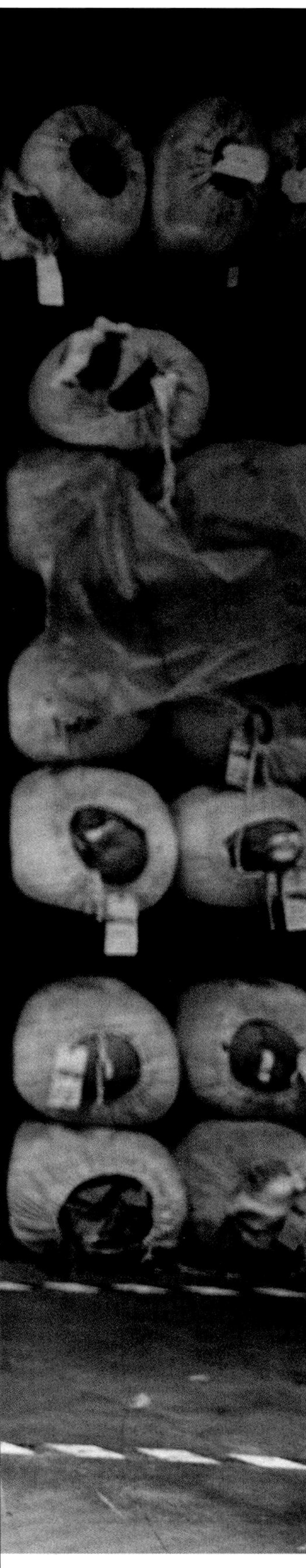

The security guard is not so much guarding the cotton
as watching over the staff of this agency, who would
receive the same special protection as senior civil servants
in the event of a catastrophe. Memphis, Tennessee

The carefully prepared black boxes with the standardized
cotton samples are sent throughout the world, most
recently also to China. Their contents provide the basis
for categorization according to color and the degree
of contamination.

One of the two US banknote printing plants is in
Fort Worth, near Dallas. The dollar bill is made up of
70 percent cotton and 30 percent linen.

One Family
One Nation
One God

Shinyanga
Mwamishali
TANZANIA
Dodoma
Morogoro
Dar Es Salaam
Mahenge

PAMBA

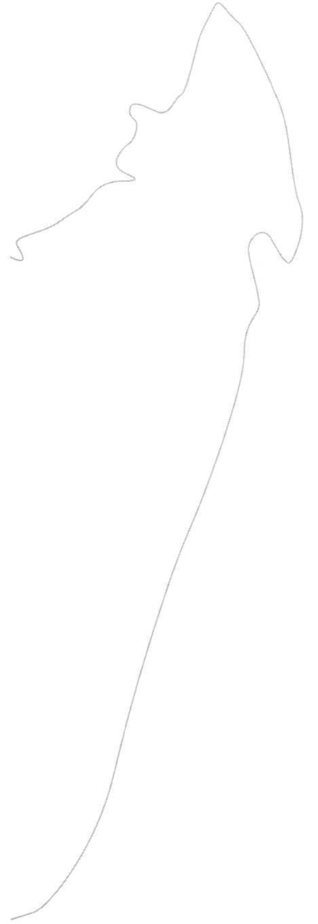

"Three years before the great
famine, the Maasai came a second
time to steal our cattle."

"Three years before the great famine, the Maasai came a second time to steal our cattle." With his strong black hands, Lela Saidai supports himself on his staff with its thick knob at one end. "About one year later I was born." He sits on a low wooden stool in front of the circular area where the cattle sleep at night, surrounded by thorny scrub. The pattern of the brushstrokes on the carefully swept ground extends across the red sand like an ornament. We are in the Meatu district, between the Shinyanga cotton center and the famous Serengeti National Park. This is where the Swiss firm bioRe has its training center. The company has been producing organic cotton since 1994, with the number of farmers involved constantly growing. Today there are around 2,400 of them. The head of training, Faustin Magallata, who is about sixty, translates with some amusement the efforts of the farmers to guess his age. He has to think somewhat longer about the number of his children. Counting on the fingers of both hands, he eventually arrives at a result: "twenty-five," but one of the young men standing behind him is more precise and says that his father has seven sons and two daughters by two wives, and that the remainder of the children he is referring to are grandchildren.

Lela Saidai lives near Nghoboko, one of the Ujamaa villages that were founded as part of the policies of Julius Nyerere, who became president of Tanzania when the country gained independence in 1961. In Tanzania's de facto national language, Swahili, *ujamaa* means "extended family" or "familyhood." Together with *urafiki* ("friendship"), it characterizes the ideology of this president, venerated by all, who wished to weave together socialist structures with the family- and clan-based traditions of Africa. Starting in 1968, the farmers were to live and produce crops together, in a model based on Soviet collective farms and Chinese rural communes. In return, the government offered them a guaranteed purchase price for their cotton, as well as schools and medical care. But the idealistic hopes of the president, who wanted to do everything better than the German and English colonial rulers had, could not last. The farmers did not want to live in the small mud huts strung out like railway cars along the sand tracks, and they often never received the money for their cotton harvests. Too great was the corruption in the state agency responsible for controlling the fortunes of this branch in all areas, from

In Africa, Tanzania is regarded as a country with
a relatively stable democracy. Political manifesto at
the Urafiki Market. Dar es Salaam

sowing to export. It has existed under various names and forms of organization since 1952, and currently operates as the Tanzania Cotton Board (TCB), with its headquarters in the country's capital city, Dar es Salaam. From the early 1980s on, trade and subsidy policies at the international level contributed to a situation in which the world market price of cotton sank below production costs. New loans had to be repeatedly taken out to balance deficits, which finally led to the collapse of the entire branch in 1985, a scenario reminiscent of the present situation in Mali. For Lela this collapse was a blessing in disguise. "We were able to return to the savanna," he recalls, and one can still sense his relief when he looks around his property. Five residential and storage buildings lie scattered among the trees, and the family members again live and work as their ancestors did: the children drive the herds of animals for miles to graze across the dry land, the women dig for water in the dried-up riverbeds, and the men build houses of mud bricks and plow the fields. In Nghoboko, the only reminder of the era of the collective farms is the central storage building, in which bioRe staff are distributing seed to the farmers contracted to produce for the Swiss organization. Sowing begins with the onset of the "small rain," the first of the two waves of monsoon rains.

"We plant thirty-seven acres with organic cotton, the remainder with corn, millet, and sunflowers," says Lela, listing some of the farm's statistics. With almost 200 acres of land, he ranks among the medium-sized farmers of his district. He does not know any more details and refers us to Happyness, one of bioRe's agricultural extension workers. Like her colleagues, Happyness looks after fifty or so farmers. Each of her visits is documented in the carefully filled columns of her field diary: each recommendation about how to deal with an attack of pests, about crop rotation, and use of fertilizer. "Lela harvested 23,765 pounds of raw cotton this year, and we purchased 19,840 pounds," as only this quantity met the criteria for export-quality cotton as laid down by the TCB.

We ask the farmer why he plants organic cotton. "There are no problems with payment and my sons have learned a great deal about agriculture." Happyness is visibly proud of this statement. Every day she visits five of *her* farmers. It is a strenuous schedule, for they all live far apart and she has to cover these distances on her bicycle. A number of her colleagues are second-generation organic farmers, who have profited from the social initiatives that the bioRe Foundation supports locally in addition to the cotton business, and which, since 2007, it has supported in collaboration with FLO-CERT. The social initiatives provide an ongoing way of checking and improving the conditions guaranteed by the Fair Trade certificate. In periods of drought these farmers did not go hungry—they had clean drinking water and were able to attend school regularly. As a result, several of them have set up small businesses, leasing land and hiring people with less education or training to plant the cotton for them. Since Nyerere's resignation in 1985, the level of education in Tanzania has declined, along with the life expectancy of the population, plagued as it is by AIDS and malaria.

"What is the next important step after plowing?" Like an elementary school teacher, Mr. Magalatta patiently questions a group of farmers who have gathered on Lela's field for training. "Compost must be spread," comes the correct answer. The next question, "What do you plant in a field in which cotton was grown the previous year?" also elicits the right response: "Millet or sunflowers." It is as if this question-and-answer game had been rehearsed for our benefit. Most of the farmers stick to the rules, and the bioRe staff are there to confirm this, as far as possible. Even so, the training center in Mwamishali has pinned up a long list of the grounds on which people can be expelled from the organization. The use of pesticides is at the top of the list. Lela Saidai is one of the contract farmers who, in return for the support they get from bioRe, sell their cotton harvest exclusively to the organization. Not all the farmers are quite as reliable as Lela, though. "Some competitors beat us to the harvest by bringing crates of Coca Cola to the farmers' doors." Cooled soft drinks are a luxury in Tanzania, where most of the houses in the steppes and savannas have no electricity. "These dealers pay more than we do, even though we add an organic premium onto the average price." The higher price offered by the dealers does not seem to make business sense, and bioRe staff members have found that the scales used by the dealers differ from those of bioRe by up to 10 percent—in the dealers' favor, of course. The farmers do not know what "price calculations" and "farm management" mean. "We are dealing with a rural population that believes in the omnipotence of rain. This is why, traditionally, they do not use fertilizer." And when the yield declines? "Then they take a fresh area of land."

Despite the common belief that there is enough land in Africa, many farmers have to leave their ancestral regions and move south to Morogoro or further, to Mahenge. In both these places the Shindika Group is active, an organization headed by Fred Shindika, the son of a retired high-ranking official of the state cotton agency. He was trained in Memphis, Tennessee, and has sixteen years' experience with European cotton dealers, the best prerequisites for getting to the top in Tanzania, both politically and socially. He not only knows the situation of Tanzanian cotton but also understands the mentality of his European-trained business partners. That, along with a well-structured business plan, ensured him the support of a Swiss development aid group in reactivating cotton cultivation in the Morogoro Rural area. "bioRe? Never heard of it," he claims, in his air-conditioned office. He has postponed our meeting three times, but now tries to make us forget this by giving us a particularly hearty welcome. The Shindika Group has exclusive purchasing rights with a good 4,000 cotton farmers, a monopoly that protects Fred Shindika from the dealers who try to poach harvests away from bioRe. "We pay decidedly more than the minimum price laid down by the state," says this bright scion of the Tanzanian upper class. We inquire what would happen if he did not do this. Given that he has a monopoly, who or what could prevent him from paying a lower price? "The farmers would resist"—of that he is convinced. "They check the world market price on the Internet and if they feel they're being badly treated they immediately call the Cotton Board to complain." In our mind's eye we picture mud huts without electricity, and Internet cafés that charge half the daily wage of a cotton picker for just one hour of surfing. But Fred Shindika refuses to be put off by this and pulls out another trump card intended to satisfy European partners: glossy brochures hot off the press inform us that in 2009 precisely 4,209 famers will produce exactly 3,800 tons of organic raw cotton. But by the end of 2008, not a single farmer had even begun to sow organic cotton. And while, with an air of doubt, we put the brochure among our documents, he has already moved on to the next topic: "Tanzania's opportunity lies in irrigated, genetically manipulated cotton. You'll see, we won't have to wait long for the permit!"

One hundred an eighty-six miles further south, after a difficult journey on unpaved roads, on car ferries, and across mountains covered in tropical rain forest, we reach Mahenge. Here, with the approval of the government, the forest is being cleared for new fields, an unexpected image that reminds us of Brazil. "What church do you work for?" is the question we get asked again and again, and Salum Mndembo, the chairman of Ulanga District Council, displays an astonishing persistence in his refusal to accept that we have no funds in our pockets for his region, which (almost) everyone has forgotten about. The sight of *mzungus*—white people—who are neither missionaries nor big-game hunters is too unfamiliar here for him to believe us. "We've been waiting for people like you to come along," he says, and then without further ado decides to send us, together with a member of the agricultural department, a jeep, and a driver, to Mwaya to study the lives of the farmers there.

They have no plows and therefore hoe their fields by hand before sowing. Electricity will not be installed in Mwaya until the following year, and the diesel-operated cotton gin remains a kind of Sleeping Beauty that will probably never wake up again. But the farmers here are used to greater difficulties: as a result of a cotton dealer's bankruptcy they are still waiting to be paid for the harvest of 2007, and so now they refuse to hand over the bales that they have carried to the storehouses on their heads or by bicycle unless they are paid straightaway. Just like their fields, which are seldom larger than a couple of acres, the sums they are paid by the buyer for the Shindika Group are paltry: 50, 70, or 100 euros. The men are happy, though. They finally have cash again and can buy new clothes at the *mitumba* market to replace those that are hanging from them in shreds. This was not always possible in the past.

"Just fifteen years ago, many colleagues came to work without a shirt to their backs and in threadbare pants," recalls Mr. Dilonga, a longtime staff member of the Tanzania-China Friendship Textile Co. Ltd. From his office window he can see the hustle and bustle across the street at Dar es Salaam's Urafiki Market, where jeans, bras, and sneakers hang in the many small stands, tidily sorted according to producer, brand, and size. "*Mitumba* is no competition for us," he says, assessing the flourishing trade in secondhand clothing from those parts of the world where people can afford to put completely intact apparel in the used-clothes collection. For his factory produces *kangas*—traditional cotton cloths printed with maxims and images relating to all situations in life, which women in Tanzania wear as wraparound skirts. "This will remain the case for quite some time," he says, sure of himself, "although young people tend to prefer European and American fashions." For one euro they can get a pair of jeans and a T-shirt, for six euros a brand-name pair of pants from England. The pants Mr. Dilonga wears are also *mitumba*, as the choice of affordable new, fashionable clothes in his country is very limited. Typewriters rattle away in the hall of his antiquated office; there is not a computer to be seen. On the wall behind the desk hangs a portrait of Nyerere, who would rather have seen his people naked than dressed in hand-me-downs from the capitalist world. Trade in these coveted goods became legal only after his resignation in 1985.

Moving past the guards and stone lions which stand protectively in front of the factory, we leave behind us the Chinese-Tanzanian friendship, which is under considerable strain because of tension between the staff from both countries. Amid the crush of the crowd at the Urafiki Market, we begin our search for Geoffrey Melonge, a *mitumba* dealer we know from Pietra Rivoli's book *The Travels of a T-Shirt in the Global Economy.* Geoffrey's story ends in 2003 in the book, and we would very much like to know how it continued to the end of 2008. There is a a small photograph of him in the book and we are immediately surrounded by inquisitive people who want to have a look at it. "I know him," one of them suddenly calls out, "but he's not here any more. He's on Kongo Road in the Kariakoo district, right in the center of town." In this part of town it is not difficult to find members of the Melonge family, which now runs a veritable *mitumba* empire. Geoffrey's brothers supervise the employees in various stores as they inventory the merchandise. Geoffrey himself is the managing director of the family-owned import company for used clothing from Great Britain.

"The best quality comes from England, and our customers know this," he explains. "For them, cheap goods from China are not a real alternative: *Mbibo our mdoshi*—which roughly translates as "Poor, always wears badly." Everyone in the trade, whether buyer or seller, can immediately tell an original from a Chinese copy. He happily remembers Pietra Rivoli and her visit to Dar es Salaam. Visibly touched, he looks at his photograph in the book: "Yes, the bale-opening parties of the Indians! We had to buy a ticket to get in." What followed was a feverish search for the best items of clothing, that sometimes turned into a brawl. "The junior head of Mohammed Enterprises is a member of parliament," Geoffrey tells us, his voice filled with admiration. "His father, Mohammed, was one of the first to travel to the villages and sell *mitumba*." There, just announcing that "We have *mitumba*" indicated the level of development and cosmopolitanism of the village.

The era of the parties is over; the Indians got out of the business once the goods began to cost money. In the past they came free from Europe and America, in the form of donations from churches and aid organizations, but today they are pre-sorted and cost Geoffrey thirty-five pounds sterling per 100-pound bale, an additional 1,350 euros in import tax per container, plus "bribes for the customs officials, otherwise I have to wait weeks for my goods."

It is still a real occasion when the goods finally arrive from the port. Privileged customers are given the first look at the merchandise, and fifty of the 500 bales that fill one container are generally sold on the very first day. "Many go to the Congo-Kinshasa and Malawi, on account of the conflicts there." Although it is an informal branch of the economy, trading in *mitumba* is at least as important for Tanzania as the production of cotton itself. The city administration in Dar es Salaam is acknowledging this fact with the construction of the Karumé Mitumba Shopping Mall, a complex several stories high. But Geoffrey is not interested in it: "The expense of checking up on the people is too great. In Africa you just can't trust anybody." In the future he plans to import cement, a rare and expensive product in Tanzania. And once he has cement, he will build an office building and business premises on Kongo Road. "It will be finished in four years at the latest. On the ground floor we will have our own sales outlet, and we will rent the upper level to the *machingas.*"

Mr. Jamal is a *machinga,* a street seller: six days a week he carries his entire business capital, consisting on average of twelve pairs of pants, under his arm through the administration center of the city. His regular customers are government and bank employees for whom dapper, European-style clothing is a must. Jamal knows both their clothing size and particular tastes, and when he has something suitable he takes it along to their office for them to try on. "At good times, like right now, I sell five to ten pairs of pants every day," he says with a note of satisfaction in his voice, as Christmas is coming and everyone wants to travel home well dressed or taking valuable presents with them. Only about one third of Tanzanians are Christian, but the legacy of the German and English colonialists still influences the rhythm of the week and the holiday seasons in the country. Jamal himself is a Muslim, and during the Friday prayer at one o'clock in the afternoon he leaves his selection of pants in the care of good friends. After that, business resumes, as it is not yet the weekend. He has no fixed stall, no license, and no tax number, and must always be on the lookout for police raids. He gets his pants for 3.50 euros a pair from middlemen, who are among Geoffrey Melonge's customers, and sells them for two to three times the price. On a good day that can bring him as much as 45 euros, a considerable sum in Tanzania, where factory workers and dockhands earn only two euros a day. Jamal is therefore satisfied with his life, which he shares with a wife and two children. He would never return to the village of his parents and their life as cashew nut farmers. He rents a small apartment on the outskirts of the city. "Two rooms," he tells us proudly. "We share the toilet with others, and we get our water from the yard," which is also where meals are cooked over an open fire. He only has one major wish left, his own 1,100-pound bale: "There is a sure profit of 175 euros to be made there." But such a bale costs almost three times this amount, an impossible sum. And then there would be the additional difficulty of where to store the goods safely.

For this he would need a stall like the one belonging to Alafani Abdu Hassani. But what Alafani has most of at present is fear.

Together with his wife, Christine, he lives near the Urafiki Market on a property that he inherited from his mother, in a tiny mud hut in which there is just enough room for a bed, a wardrobe, and a table. Under the low corrugated metal roof the heat is oppressive, the room almost pitch dark. "We don't leave the light on at night, otherwise hands reach out for us." There are beads of sweat on his brow. "And black cats, as big and heavy as humans, jump onto the roof." The panic in his face is genuine, as is the agitation when he tells us about the witchcraft that has been threatening him and his wife for the last three years. "Christine lost our child, my mother and one of my sisters went mad and died, I myself was close to death," all proof that his brothers and sisters have cast a spell on him. The bone of contention is money and the construction of a house several stories high on a site that belonged to his mother in the urban Mahenge district, which thirty years ago was still farmland. Behind a torn poster of Tanzania's current president, Jakaya Kikwete, who looks out earnestly from above the couple's bed, Alafani hides the documents that he hopes will lead to a court ruling in his favor. He is forty years old, his wife twelve years younger. She sits calmly on the only unoccupied piece of the floor and watches her husband take out one document after another. Then he begins to weep. He can no longer work, he murmurs, can no longer fight against this evil. "I fetched a mullah, who prayed with me here in the yard, and I went to the Christians as well." He welcomes any support he is given. The women's clothing that Alafani sells looks as outmoded and unkempt as the stall itself and seems to reflect the owner's state of mind. "We can hardly live on what I earn here," which is hardly suprising as "the evil drives the customers away." We give him money to photocopy his documents for his court case, which will take place soon. There is little use in arguing against the existence of witchcraft, as it is real for those who believe in it. Alafani becomes indignant at comments implying this. "But I'm not the one who believes in this evil," he cries. "It's my brothers and sisters who send it to me!"

A little while later we see a woman sitting in an overcrowded minibus on its way to the center of Dar es Salaam. A hat casts a shadow across her face, her sensitive eyes are hidden by thick glasses. Her skin is white and chapped, yet her facial features are otherwise those of her fellow Tanzanians: this woman is one of the many albinos in Africa. Every day there are newspaper reports about the murder of albinos, about how they are literally hunted down, their graves desecrated, and their corpses plundered—because their bones and hair are believed to help achieve power and wealth. The instigators of these acts are the witch doctors.

Mitumba, second-hand clothing from Europe and America, is to be found in even the remotest of villages. Trading in these goods has been legal since 1985, when the first president, Julius Nyerere, resigned. Mahenge

APENDANAO NI SISI HEBU TUPENI NAFAS

Since 1994, the Swiss business bioRe has assisted a growing number of farmers near Shinyanga in the Meatu district with the production of organic cotton. Training is also given directly on the fields. Mwanhuzi near Mwamishali

Extension worker Happyness and her colleagues each supervise around fifty farmers. She is proud of the positive response to her work. Many of her clients are contract farmers of bioRe, because of the assistance the Swiss firm offers. Nghoboko near Mwamishali

With the death of her husband, Kundi Ngasa, 47, was not
only left widowed. She also lost her property to his family.
With two cows that she inherited from her father, she
was able to buy twelve and a half acres of land, which she
has worked for seven years with the help of her nephew.
Almost half of her land is planted with organic cotton.
Near Mwanhuzi

In 1995, Malunde Sele was one of the first to plant organic
cotton. He proudly displays a photograph that shows
him in 2001 with the founder of bioRe. Near Mwanhuzi

Plowing can be carried out after the first "small" rainfall
at the end of November.

The TCB (Tanzania Cotton Board) requires farmers
to remove the dried-up cotton plants after the
harvest. This minimizes the survival chances of pests.
Near Mwanhuzi

In some areas of Tanzania, like in Mwaya, near Mahenge, plows are unknown.

Calabashes of all sizes are to be found in almost every Tanzanian household. Near Mwanhuzi

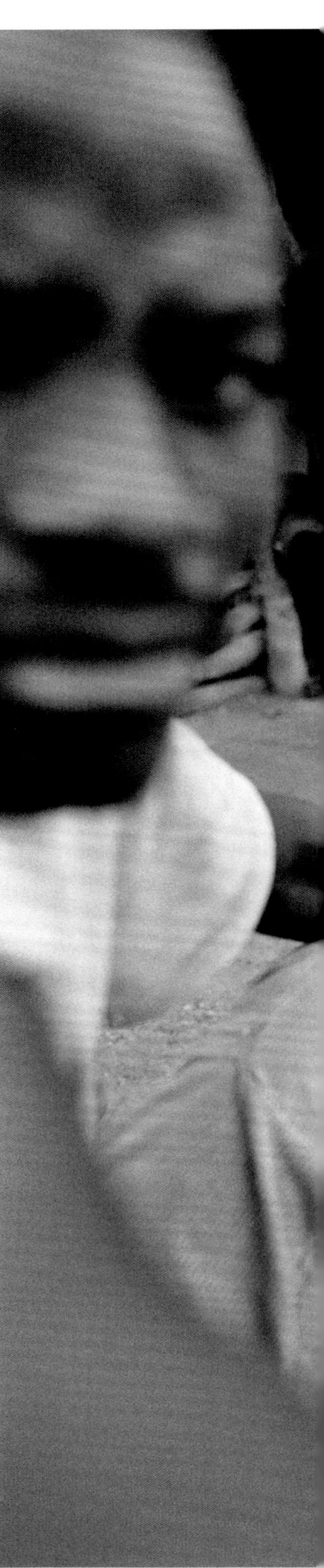

Staff members of bioRe hand out the seed for the new
season. In contrast to their fellow farmers who are
supplied by the Cotton Board, the contract farmers do
not have to pay for it. Nghoboko near Mwanhuzi

Haji Masudi, in the center of the photo, is the Mwaya
Division Secretary and also responsible for cotton. He hopes
that his villages will be provided with electricity next year.
The cotton gin in Mwaya had always been run on generators,
but has been standing idle for years because of the high
price of diesel. Mwaya near Mahenge

"Some competitors beat us to the
harvest by bringing crates of Coca Cola
to the farmers' doors."

The involvement of the bioRe Stiftung (foundation) in health
and education services is bearing fruit: a number of the
workers who are on their way to consultations in the villages
are the children of farmers who started to cultivate organic
cotton back in the 1990s. Nghoboko near Mwanhuzi

The bales, which weigh 500 pounds, are moved
by hand and loaded onto trucks that take them
to the containers for shipping throughout the world.
Warehouse in Dar es Salaam

The Tanzania-China Friendship Textile Co. Ltd. is one of
eleven textile factories in Tanzania. It is state-owned
by China and Tanzania; the Chinese side is to be privatized
shortly. Dar es Salaam

Mr. Dilonga has worked for this company for thirty years.
He does not regard the sale of *mitumba* as competition,
as the Friendship Textile Co. mostly produces *kangas,* wrapa-
round skirts printed with maxims and images of all kinds.
He himself wears *mitumba* pants, as there are hardly any new
European-style trousers available. Dar es Salaam

Geoffrey Melonge in the storehouse of the CHATA
Investment Co. Ltd., his *mitumba* import company.
He started in the early 1990s at the Urafiki Market with
a few T-shirts and soon plans to erect a multistory
commercial building in the Kariakoo shopping district
of the inner city. Dar es Salaam

Opening the bales at the market at Karume Stadium.
The battle for the best pieces begins immediately,
as there is a great demand for brand names and designs.
Dar es Salaam

Many *mitumba* traders carry their entire business capital, in the form of prestigious European makes of pants, under their arm. Morogoro

The business of Alafani Abdu Hassani at the Urafiki Market is doing very badly. He is convinced this is because his relatives have put a jinx on him over a dispute about an inheritance. Dar es Salaam

SWEET AFRICA
QG Engineering Ltd.

After a number of bad experiences with cotton dealers, the
farmers in the district of Mwaya now demand cash payment
upon delivering their cotton to the warehouses.

Literature on the subject:

Osteuropa Grünbuch, Politische Ökologie im Osten Europas
4-5 2008 (various authors)

The Aral Sea Tragedy, Grigori Reznichenko
Novosti 1992, Moscow

Landwirtschaftliche Transformation, Desertifikation und nachhaltige
Ressourcennutzung Fallbeispiel Usbekistan, Bonn 2004,
Studies Elke Herrfahrdt

Seta e Veleni Duilio Giammaria
4.2007 Feltrinelli/Traveller

Zum Beispiel Baumwolle, Carina Weber/Dagmar Parusel
Süd-Nord Lamuv 1995

(UN)FAIR TRADE, Jean-Pierre Boris
Goldmann 2006

Fünf Pflanzen verändern die Welt, Henry Hobhouse
dtv 1.1992

Reisebericht eines T-Shirts, Pietra Rivoli
Econ 2006 ISBN

Der Streit um die Entwicklungshilfe, Peter Niggli
Rotpunktverlag 2008

Weisse Plantagen, Erik Orsenna
C.H.Beck 2007

Wir Neger in Amerika, Richard Wright
Büchergilde Gutenberg 1948

Web sites on the subject:

www.kingcotton.de
www.thrakika.gr/en/news/world
www.helvetas.ch Kompetenzzentrum Baumwolle
www.arte.tv/lemondeselonmonsanto
www.baumwollboerse.de

Further information: www.hanspeterjost.com

Our heartfelt thanks go to all the people around the world
who helped us, and without whom this book would not have
been possible.

In particular to Pietra Rivoli, Qu Lijun, Ma Jane, the Prochnow
family, John Johnson, PCCA, Datta Pattil and Aarti Pakharaj,
YUVA, Marc Traoré and Kij Kadiatou Touré, CAEB, Firdauz,
Mr. Ummar, the De Luca & De Luca photographer family, Kurt
Schmid, Beatrice Hofmann, Regine Lueg and Harald Grunwald,
Adi Theimer, and Iwan Raschle

For the financial support of the reportage we thank the
Hamasil Stiftung, the Parrotia-Stiftung, the Schwyzer-Winiker-
Stiftung, the Volkart Stiftung, Victorinox

For the financial support of the production of the book we thank
bioRe, COOP Naturaplan, Switcher, the Kulturstiftung Winterthur,
the Stiftung der Schweizerischen Landesausstellung 1939,
the Dr. Georg und Josi Guggenheim Stiftung, and Victorinox

COTTON worldwide

Photographie: Hans Peter Jost, text: Christina Kleineidam
Idea and concept: Hans Peter Jost
Design: Integral Lars Müller with Hans Peter Jost
Translation: Roderick O'Donovan
Copyediting: Rita M. Forbes, Danko Szabo, Munich
Coordination: Katharina Kulke
Production: Amelie Solbrig
Printing and Binding: EBS Bortolazzi STEI, Verona/Italy

ISBN 978-3-03778-201-9
ISBN 978-3-03778-200-2 German

© 2010 Lars Müller Publishers

Lars Müller Publishers
Baden, Switzerland
www.lars-muller-publishers.com

Printed in Italy

Also available:
From Somewhere to Nowhere, China's Internal Migrants,
Andreas Seibert, 978-3-03778-146-3
The Face of Human Rights, Walter Kälin, Lars Müller,
Judith Wyttenbach (eds), 978-3-03778-017-6
Who owns the Water? Lars Müller, Klaus Lanz, Christian Rentsch und
Réne Schwarzenbach (eds) with the support of EAWAG, 978-3-03778-018-3